To Lesley

B&B

THE BOOK OF BREAKFAST & BRUNCH
BY HUGO WOOLLEY

Best of Breakfasts

Hugo

_Breakfast and brunch are the best meals of
the day – who has ever heard of an 'All Day Lunch'?!_

ISBN & PUBLISHING DETAILS

Publishing Details:

Breakfast Book
First published in Great Britain 2006 by: Breakfast Book Ltd.
Woodlands Country House, Cornwall PL28 8RU.
Copyright © Breakfast, HUGO WOOLLEY 2006 Breakfast Book Ltd.
ISBN # 978-0-9555930-0-0
Written and Illustrated: Hugo Woolley

Brunch Book
First published in Great Britain 2007 by: Breakfast Book Ltd.
Woodlands Country House, Cornwall PL28 8RU
Copyright © HUGO WOOLLEY 2007, Breakfast Book Ltd.
ISBN # 978-0-9555930-1-7
Written and Illustrated: Hugo Woolley

B&B – Breakfast and Brunch
First published in Great Britain 2009 by:
Breakfast Book Ltd. Woodlands Country House, Treator, Padstow PL28 8RU
Breakfast Book Ltd. B&B Copyright © Hugo Woolley 2009

ISBN # 978-0-9555930-2-4

Printed and designed: Hudson Armstrong Design. www.hudsonarmstrong.com
Written and illustrated: Hugo Woolley. www.breakfastbook.co.uk
Photo of Hugo Woolley: Mark Rushton

A MESSAGE FROM RICK STEIN

"It's great reading this book – 'Breakfast and Brunch' – as it is amusing as well as having some lovely recipes. Hugo has a strange sense of humour and some of these dishes are rather bizarre... Fried worms is typical of him and the Spicy Beef Burritos must be famous for their lingering afterburn, right up my street as it happens. Indeed I'm going to make Hugo's fruit salad dressing with a dash of red chilli powder like they do in Vera Cruz. This reminds me of the most bizarre breakfast I had early one morning in Mexico, a cup of hot chocolate and cinnamon and a little bag of freshly fried grasshoppers with salt and chilli outside the Benito Juárez Market in Oaxaca".

Best wishes,

Rick.

'When you wake up in the morning, Pooh,' said Piglet at last,
'what's the first thing you say to yourself?'
'What's for breakfast' said Pooh. 'What do you say, Piglet?'
'I say, I wonder what's going to happen exciting today' said Piglet.
Pooh nodded thoughtfully. 'It's the same thing,' he said.
A. A. Milne, 'The House at Pooh Corner'

CONTENTS

V = Vegetarian   GF = Gluten Free   DF = Dairy Free

BREAKFAST - THE MOST IMPORTANT MEAL OF THE DAY...

Somebody once said; 'Breakfast is the most important meal of the day'. The day should start with a good breakfast. It not only invigorates your intelligence; it lowers stress and (believe it or not) keeps the weight down – even reduces it! I have been reliably informed that, a good bit of cholesterol in the morning gets rid of suicidal tendencies – however – it was a dairy farmer who told me this! Breakfast should be eaten leisurely, at a table with a newspaper to read to prevent hurried consumption, also an array of condiments scattered around to complement this essential meal. This is a feast eaten in silence, with a trickle of music from the radio in the background, only the near noiseless and polite acknowledgment to your loved one or guest, when they appear. Never eat your breakfast on the hoof unless you are camping or picnicking. Eating breakfast on the way to work will only give you indigestion or, a dollop of tomato sauce on your tie or egg on your face.

Breakfasts around the world differ in style, content and volume. The one we in England think of is 'The Full English' – basically, a fry-up of sausage, bacon, black-pudding, baked tomato, mushrooms and a variety of eggs on fried bread possibly some baked beans. The Scots have porridge, then a fry-up, the Welsh have a 'Full English' (well – Welsh, I suppose) but with the addition of Larva Bread and Cockles! And the Northern Irish enjoy a Potato Boxdy (a potato cake) with their fry-up or 'Ulster Fry'. The French dip Croissants into their bowls of coffee and eat delicate fluffy pastries and smoke a cigarette, that is all they have for breakfast and then a 3 hour lunch. The Americans, however, have everything from Waffles to 'Breakfast Casserole' in the morning (and something called Grits; which I'd rather not go into!). The Americans have made breakfast into a virtual science and they do it terribly well – sometimes. However, it is acknowledged, world-wide, that a British breakfast, is the finest!

In Bermuda, salt cod is eaten quite a lot for breakfast as well as a rather tasteless fish pasty (it might have just been the way the hotel we stayed at, cooked them). Thailand (and I suspect in China as well) – according to my son who spent a lot of time there on a 'Gap' year – enjoy exotic fruits, with a kind of savoury doughnut and a rice porridge with coconut milk. India has curried potato and pea parcels, deep fried, or fermented rice cakes and lots of delicious tea. The North Europeans enjoy sliced meats and cheeses and lots of cream, yoghurt, heavy black rye bread and butter – they don't have much in the way of cooked breakfasts except the coastal towns enjoy fried herring. This is where the fish is freshest – fresh off the boats. My friend Dave, a Padstow fisherman (who also has a B&B), treats his guests to fresh mackerel fillets, dusted in flour and fried gently in butter. Very simple but for best results, the mackerels have to be as fresh as fresh can be from the sea, caught at least the day before! The advantages of a fisherman and B&B owner, I suppose. He has also been known to give his guests Lobster for breakfast!

Nearly everybody can make breakfast – if they can't – it is very easy to learn. Hopefully this book will inspire you to make a great breakfast. There are Breakfasts that are good for you, substantial, light or fruity, spicy or creamy, some to sort out a hangover, or a work of art to eat late on Sunday morning with the papers and listening to The Archers (for unfamiliar readers; the Archers are farming folk depicted in a radio 'soap' – something some of us Brits have been listening to for the past forty years!) There are ideas for quick breakfasts and breakfasts you prepare the night before.

To eat well in England you should have breakfast three times a day.
Somerset Maugham

BRUNCH - A MORE SOPHISTICATED BREAKFAST...

I believe this is an American invention for a meal, as the name would imply, to be eaten in-between or instead of breakfast and lunch. This is a feast, usually informal – pyjamas and dressing gowns can be worn, at leisure, on Sundays with the papers and/or on holiday. It is more substantial than an early morning breakfast (well, mine are) and may go to two or three courses! Starter – main course – toast and jam or a 'puddingy' thing. These days, it is quite fashionable to have 'Brunch Meetings' in the City offices where the moguls of business can wheel and deal without the inconvenience of getting up early to slot in a hurried breakfast. Nothing appals me more than discussing business over breakfast, it can't be good for you, but Brunch is slightly different.

You do not rush a Brunch! It should be regarded as more of a party meal. Talking at Brunch is more permissible than at Breakfast. But, you should gage the mood of the other 'Brunchers' before launching into a diatribe about your 'goings on' of the previous evening or your latest holiday adventures!

Some of these recipes I enjoy, not only for Brunch but also for supper. I have included some snacks that are traditionally eaten in the very early hours; Breakfast eaten before you go to bed (if you go to bed at all!), after the last waltz has been played and you are beginning to sober up. These are more 'snacky' and could be called a 'Latefast'. The classic 'Latefast' dish is a thick Bacon Roll with a fried egg, Tabasco sauce and lots of butter.

I cook on a four-oven Aga and you will find most of the Breakfasts and Brunches that require baking use only a couple of temperatures – 180°C or 230°C (bottom-right or top-right Aga oven). Fan-ovens cook a little warmer and you will have to reduce the temperatures by at least 20°C.

The poor old French and other Europeans have, in my experience, a terrible attitude to Breakfast and Brunch – they are small, unimaginative breakfasts with lots of fluffy pastry. No wonder they are all so thin and take 3 hours over lunch! Breakfast and Brunch can be treated as an unimportant meal in the UK, not really taken seriously by some people, the same-old-things always turn up in the morning, dripping in fat or oil and made with second-rate produce. Take this meal seriously and you could survive through to dinner, feeling good and alert. This is, after all, a meal you can eat any time of day – unlike lunch or dinner or tea – who has ever heard of an 'all day lunch'?

The great joy of writing this book is the development of the recipes both traditional and innovative. I have had a lot of support from people like Rick Stein (to 'drop' a name) and all our friends in Padstow, Cornwall; from friends and relations aboard and fellow 'Breakfast Enthusiasts' and B&B owners. Unfortunately, I always make a terrible mess and it is my wife, Pippa, who is the one that always seems to end up cleaning my surfaces up whilst I am setting up the photo, writing the recipes or going on to a new dish. It is mainly thanks to her patience 'Breakfast & Brunch' comes to you! This book, I hope will inspire you to an adventurous Breakfast – impress a loved one, or an important guest or an in-law or two. You will get an immense amount of satisfaction and Brownie Points!

He that but looketh on a plate of ham and eggs to lust after it hath already committed breakfast with it in his heart.

C.S. Lewis

SUPPLIERS & PRODUCERS

A good breakfast relies on the products you use. No matter how much care you take in preparing your breakfast, it will be mediocre – if not inedible – if you use second-rate, cheap, over processed or spoiled ingredients.

I have sprinkled suggestions throughout the book as to where to buy the best local ingredients. Books like Rick Stein's Food Heroes are also a great help. Take a bit of time and research the best place to get sausages and bacon – there are still a lot of little butchers who cure their own bacon (mine even grows his own Gloucester Old Spot pigs). They should hand-link their own sausages with real skins and only use proper cuts of sows (female pig) meat to make the sausage-meat.

Bread is now such a difficulty, as all the old bakers seem to have disappeared. If you 'squish' a slice of supermarket bread in your hand it will go into a sort of doughy lump and not spring back! And check it is not full of added salt. If you have a local baker, hold on to him/her for dear life; support them and use their product! Making one's own bread is quite easy with bread machines – and very satisfying.

Good eggs are quite easy to get hold of. The ones you buy from the farm gate are probably the best but, unfortunately, there are some unscrupulous people who buy cheap eggs from the supermarket and re-pack them as their own! The big give away is they are date-stamped – farm-gate eggs will probably not be or if they are; they will have been laid a day or so ago. Supermarkets have a good selection nowadays but are seldom fresh or British – that is; laid-the-day-before-fresh, good butchers usually sell the local farmer's eggs. See the Egg chapter – page 36.

Local is always better – but only if it is excellent! There is no point of buying local for the sake of it – it has to be good quality, it will not have travelled miles, sat in a holding depot for ages, picked or cropped early so by the time it gets to the supermarket it's ripe. "Vine ripened" seems to be today's 'buzz words', but is it "vine ripened" if a bit of twig is attached to it; but picked 6 days ago in Spain and ripened in the lorry!? Dairy products last longer and generally taste better from the dairy round the corner (sadly, only for country dwellers). And one's own tomatoes or herbs are a great satisfaction and are far sweeter and tastier better than the 'forced', flabby stuff in supermarket pots. In London, I used to have boxes of parsley on the kitchen window and tomatoes grew very well in the little yard at the back of the house. There are some wonderful farmers markets in London and Birmingham that I know about; I know there is one in Tunbridge Wells in Kent as I was part of its beginnings – I think there are Markets in all the other big urban areas. Farmers Markets and farm shops are a great place to find lovely local foods, especially breakfast stuff. So, you can find decent, un-processed products in towns as well as in the countryside. There is no excuse to buy cheap processed products; your breakfast will not be cheaper, just shrivelled up, tasteless, full of salt and preservatives and probably unhealthy!

Sausages: There are five things to remember when you are choosing a sausage.

(1) Make sure that the minimum meat content is over 70%, preferably 80 to 90%, the percentage will be shown on the packet or label. (2) Sausages should have proper skins, not fake ones but natural skins – 'Casings' (as they are called in the trade). (3) The meat in the sausages should be made with prime cuts of (preferably sow's) meat, usually shoulder, belly or leg. You can tell if they have got left-overs in them (head meat and mechanically recovered meat, are the rather unsavoury technical terms) they are bright, rose pink (that's colouring,) there is not a speckled meaty look about them, instead, they are all the same smooth colour like pink mashed potato. And the big give away is if they are cheap. A proper sausage should cost a little more than pork chops per pound (or Kilo.) You have got to wonder what part of the animal is being used if it is cheap! (4) There should only be the minimum of additives not lots of different 'E' numbers. Avoid sausages with colouring and unnatural things that you would not expect in a sausage like "gua gum" or yeast extract or anything else you have not heard of. Saltpetre you will find in Continental sausages and gives that rather characteristic Continental taste – found mostly in Frankfurters and French sausages. (5) There are two ways to make a sausage: The British way uses Rusk (a kind of bread crumb) to bind the sausage together, so when you cook them, they will keep all the

juices and not all fall apart, NOT, as some people think to bulk out the meat (check out the meat content). The European way is to use pork or beef fat and the meat is generally coarser ground.

We in Britain also enjoy Black Pudding – a Blood sausage made with cereal and spices, boiled in a skin or bag, sliced and fried for the proper Full English Breakfast. In Cornwall, we enjoy a Hogs Pudding or 'Pudden'. This is also a thick pork and bread sausage, spices and herbs (sometimes), boiled then sliced and fried. (A 'Pudding' is basically meat or a cake-mix boiled in a bag – a method of cooking that has been used for hundreds of years – since Roman times). The variety of sausages is huge; however, I think, for breakfast, they should be simple, juicy pork or beef sausages with no surprises (like chilli or garlic) with a hint of sage and/or mace. Toulouse-style, chipolata sausages are very good for a Continental-type breakfast with a slice of smoked ham, eggs of your choice and some toasted Brioche.

There are some rules about cooking sausages: You must never, ever prick them or deep-fry them; it loses all the sausages' juiciness. Fry, grill or bake them gently in a pan, grill or oven with a tiny bit of oil, slowly, turning them every five minutes for at least 20 minutes.

Bacon is cured pork. This means the joints of pork meat (it can also be beef, venison and, lately, turkey) is salted – left in a container full of curing salt so that all the moisture in the meat is drawn out – this is done for quite a few days, sometimes weeks, then hung up, the salt brushed off and left to cure in the fresh air or in cool wood-smoke. Well, that is how it was done before health and safety, mass production and watery bacon became the norm! For best bacon, look for 'dry cured' with lots of fat on the rind. The rind should be left on because, when a machine takes off the rind, it takes too much of the fat with it.

Lots of butchers cure their own bacon and I think the best cut is the Collar; a loop of meaty back bacon with a bit of Streaky attached to it. Some Streaky bacon is cured in a vat of curing salts and water, then very thinly sliced and sold as American bacon. It is very good for crispy bacon because there is water in the meat. However, it shrinks terribly. For crisp, tasty bacon, get some thinly sliced Pancetta, now available in the supermarkets and the best butchers. Back bacon is very popular as there is plenty of meat, however, not very good to crisp up – the meaty bit can go like plastic. Like a sausage, cheap bacon is a false economy; it shrivels to nothing as it is cured in water to plump it out and lots of white stuff is released whilst cooking. This is the curing water. I am also unhappy by the way pork from abroad is kept. They do not have the same husbandry standards as we do and bacon that says it is processed in the UK, doesn't necessarily mean the pigs were reared in the UK. This might change in the near future as it is being seen as an obvious con!

Fish for Breakfast and Brunch is generally down to smoked fish. We are the only nation that has kippers (smoked herring). You can buy them filleted or whole with bones. I prefer to buy them whole – with bones as they are usually properly smoked. Most Kipper fillets have fake smoke painted on and I get the taste repeating on me all through the rest of the day! Smoked haddock is a wonderful fish to start the day with. Don't buy the yellow dyed haddock; it has a metallic taste and is used on sub-standard fish. Smoked salmon is very popular in the morning; again, cheap smoked salmon is sometimes dyed and this produces a metallic taste. Go for the mid-priced, un-dyed salmon. Fishcakes (page 81 & 82) are a superb start to the day – they can be made the day before with either un-smoked or smoked fish.

Making your own is not only fun and satisfying; it also can be cheaper. **Jams and marmalades** can be quite difficult - well it seems to be for me but luckily Pippa and the local WI are wonderful for homemade jams and chutneys. Telling everybody it is homemade instantly puts you above the rest. I know it takes time but if you put a good TV in the kitchen, get a good washing-up machine (instead of your wife, because you won't be popular) and a comfy stool, you will find you will have a lovely time creating wonderful Breakfasts and Brunches.

MUESLI (V)

INGREDIENTS

* = Essential items

*Rolled porridge oats – 15%
*Jumbo oats – 15%
Wheat germ for even more fibre – 5%
Malted wheat flakes or crunched up bran flakes – 15%
*Nuts – 10%
Roasted almonds – put onto a baking tray, into a hot oven for 5 minutes – keep an eye on them, they turn black in seconds if not watched
*Sultanas 5%
*Pitted prunes cut in half – 5%
Roasted Pecan nuts – cover with honey and roast in a hot oven for 3 minutes for even more sweetness or roast with maple syrup
Lexia raisins (they are wonderful, waxy plump fruit) 5%
Banana chips – slices of candied banana – 5%
Sweetened cranberries or dried strawberries – 5%
*Ready-to-eat apricots – 5%
Dried figs cut in quarters – 5%
Pumpkin seeds – 2.5%
*Sunflower seeds – 2.5%

'Knit your own' muesli, it is a fantastic start to the day, look at all those healthy Swiss! Muesli has got some bad press over the last thirty years when people first started eating it. Muesli smacked of tree-hugging hippy type vegetarians eating something like sawdust. The thing is; it is a very simple, delicious and quick way of starting the day. There are plenty of ready made mueslis but, for me, there is never enough of my favourite things or too much sweet stuff. There is usually lots of added bits and pieces to stabilise what is in the packet, like soya and salt. The health-food shop is the best place to get the ingredients. I have indicated the percentage of each ingredient, the one you don't like leave out or use an alternative:

METHOD

Mix all these ingredients together, add more or take out your least favourite things. Store in an airtight container for a week or two. *Indicates essential items in a muesli for good health and good muesli. Chop fresh fruit into your muesli, drench with milk, sprinkle with sugar or pour on honey or maple syrup – or nothing sweet at all. If you double the percentage and change into grams, this will give you a good portion: example 2.5% X 2 = 5 therefore 5 grams. Takes one back to school, doesn't it?!

Alternatively: mix in lots of yoghurt and/or milk or Soya milk (if dairy intolerant) with maple syrup or honey the night before. Leave in the fridge and in the morning chop in some seasonal fresh fruit – apple, summer berries, banana, pineapple etc, the muesli becomes a sort of cold, fruity porridge. Fantastically good for you – and very Swiss.

GRANOLA (V, DF)

INGREDIENTS

For a large bowl-full to keep one person going for a week:

2 tablespoons vegetable oil or clarified butter

125ml (5fl oz) warm water

3 tablespoons honey

3 tablespoons golden syrup

1 teaspoon vanilla extract

A pinch of salt

300g (12oz) Jumbo oats – porridge oats won't do for this recipe

100g (4oz) each: flaked almonds, desiccated coconut, sunflower seeds, pumpkin seeds, sesame seeds, and chopped pecan or walnuts

1 teaspoon ground cinnamon

100g (4oz) each: chopped dried apricots or sweetened dried cranberries and large Australian golden sultanas or any plump dried fruit

The grated zest of ½ an orange

Granola has its origins in America with the influences from North European immigrants. Similar to baked Muesli but with more in the way of nuts and seeds and sweetened with honey and/or Maple syrup and golden syrup. This recipe is not too sweet – some granola; mainly the proprietary brands, are so sweet, it is positively sickly (for us over 40 that is).

METHOD

Heat the oven to 230°C, 450°F, gas mark 8.

Mix the oil, warm water, honey, syrup, and vanilla essence together in a jug until the honey and syrup melts in with the water. In a large mixing bowl, mix the oats, almonds, coconut, seeds, nuts, and ground cinnamon and mix everything well. Pour over the sweetening mixture and mix together. When everything is thoroughly coated and slightly moistened (hate that word), tip it all out onto a large baking sheet or two baking sheets so that there is a thin layer of Granola on the sheet. Bake in the centre of the hot oven for 5 minutes, if you have two trays, put one in the centre and one on the top shelf of the oven, after 5 minutes, take out the trays, give them a mix so that all the Granola is toasted, then, put the trays back, swapping them from top to centre so that they get an equal toasting for another five minutes. Mix the granola and place the trays in the oven for a further 10 to 15 minutes, mixing every 5 minutes until the Granola is toasted a gold-brown and dry.

Remove from the oven and pour the granola into a dry, big mixing bowl and mix in the dried fruit and orange zest. Allow to cool. When the Granola is cool, put into an air-tight container. You can store the Granola like this for 2 or 3 weeks.

If you like things even sweeter add 4 to 6 tablespoons maple syrup and use a little less water. Serve with a little milk or apple and/or orange juice, or a couple tablespoons low-fat yoghurt or sprinkle over fruit salad. Granola is very good for you; it has the same nutritional value as those awful cereals that you are made to eat if you are on a high fibre diet that taste like a cross between wet cardboard and sawdust.

MARMALADE BARS (V)

INGREDIENTS

For 12 large or 24 small bars:

250g (9oz) butter

200g (7oz) light soft brown, sugar

150g (5oz) self-raising flour

350g porridge oats

3 or 4 tablespoons of your favourite marmalade – it should have thin-cut shreds and be tangy

50g (2oz) sultanas

50g (2oz) ready-to-eat, dried apricots sliced thinly, like marmalade shreds

50g (2oz) sliced almonds

About 2 tablespoons honey

It's nice to have a snack to get you going in the morning. If you are one of these strange people who can only face a cup of coffee in the morning, these are very good for you to nibble. These bars are oaty, soft, but crunchy – they are a cross between a flapjack and cake and have a little tang from the marmalade. You could survive with just a Marmalade Bar in the morning. This is so simple; you could get the children to make them for you.

METHOD

Preheat oven to 190°C, 375°F, Gas mark 5.

You need a non-stick baking pan – 32cm L X 18cm W X 3cm D.

Melt the butter in a large mixing bowl in the microwave, add the sugar. Mix in the flour and the porridge oats so that the butter and sugar covers everything and the whole lot is thoroughly mixed in.

Spoon out half the mixture into the baking pan and flatten equally over the bottom using a pallet knife. Press down the mixture, into the corners, check it is the same thickness. Now spread the marmalade over the mixture, evenly distributing the shreds. Sprinkle on the sultanas and shredded apricots. Mix in the almonds into the rest of the oats, sugar and butter and spread the mixture over the top of the marmalade and flatten out as before. Heat up some honey in the microwave so it is very liquid, brush it or drizzle it on the top of the oat mixture, it will give the bars a shine.

Place in the middle shelf of the oven and bake for 30 to 35 minutes. When it is baked, allow it to cool in the baking tray. The mixture will firm up as it cools, ready for cutting into bars or squares.

These bars will keep for a week in an air-tight container. One of our B&B guests suggested Ginger Marmalade or Lime Marmalade instead of ordinary Marmalade which I thought a great idea (unfortunately, I hate both Ginger and Lime!).

GRAPEFRUIT GRANITA (V, GF, DF)

INGREDIENTS

For 4 people or a tub to yourself!

25g (1oz) granulated sugar

600ml (1 pint) water

300ml (½ pint) fresh grapefruit juice – about 3 grapefruits. If you can get a bit of the pulp from the squeezer (about a tablespoon) it will give the Granita some texture. Try to use fresh grapefruit as carton does not make a very good Granita

2 teaspoons of grated grapefruit rind

A very refreshing water-ice for the morning. This will wake you up and inject some vitamins. Serve with a Shrewsbury Biscuit (page 16) or a Madeleine (page 33).

METHOD

Melt the sugar in the water in a saucepan, stir over a moderate heat until the sugar has dissolved then bring to the boil and boil for 5 minutes.

Cool to room temperature and add the fruit juice and stir in the zest, place onto a large, wide plastic freezer-proof tray and put into the freezer until it has turned to a soft ice, snowy texture. Stir up the crystals and put back into the freezer. Then stir up the Granita again after 30 minutes. Repeat this process a couple more times until you have a smooth, sorbet consistency. If it freezes solid, allow it to melt for half an hour out in the kitchen or two hours in the fridge and then stir it up again to the desired texture.

Serve in a Sundae Glass with Shrewsbury Biscuits. I enjoy putting in a straw so that you can suck up the juice as it melts. For extra sweetness; pour some Cassis over the top of the Granita – it produces wonderful colours as well!

Life is like a grapefruit. Well, it's sort of orangy-yellow and dimpled on the outside, wet and squidgy in the middle. It's got pips inside, too. Oh, and some people have a half a one for breakfast.

Douglas Adams

SHREWSBURY BISCUITS (V)

INGREDIENTS

For about 24 biscuits:

110g (4oz) soft butter

150g (5oz) caster sugar

1 large egg

2 teaspoons rose water

225g (8oz) plain flour

1 teaspoon baking powder

The zest of one lemon

(A tablespoon of caraway seeds – optional)

This is a very old fashioned biscuit. It is sweet, and a hint of savoury if you add caraway seeds and Rose Water which is how they are traditionally made. It compliments the sourness of grapefruit wonderfully. Serve it with Grapefruit Granita (page 15).

METHOD

Preheat oven 190°C, 375°F, gas mark 5.

Cream the butter and the sugar with a hand-whisk until pale. Gradually whisk in the egg and the rose water. Sift in the flour and baking powder and mix in with the rest of the ingredients, add the lemon zest. Mix into a fairly firm dough – add a little more flour if necessary. (Knead in the caraway seeds at this stage). Turn out the dough onto a floured surface and knead for about 2 minutes.

Roll the dough out to about 1½cm (half an inch) thick and cut into fingers about 10cm by 2cm (4 X 1 inches) and lay them on a baking sheet lined with baking parchment, at least 2cm apart. Bake the biscuits for 15 minutes, until lightly browned and firm to the touch. The biscuits will grow bigger. Cut the biscuits and lay to cool on a cooling rack. Store in an airtight container or biscuit tin.

Traditionally, Shrewsbury Biscuits have caraway seeds as well, but I am not partial to them. If you enjoy the slightly aniseed, scented taste of caraway seeds, add a tablespoon to the dough.

CINNAMON TOAST STICKS (V)

INGREDIENTS

For 18 sticks:

150g (6oz) Unsalted butter

50g (2oz) Icing sugar

50g (2oz) Demerara sugar

1 Tablespoon cinnamon

6 Slices thin white bread crusts removed and cut into 3 sticks like 'soldiers'

OR 4 thick slices 2 cm (¾ inch) from an un-sliced loaf, cut into sticks 2cm thick

These sticks are best served with coffee as an 'appetiser' for your breakfast – why shouldn't you have an appetiser for breakfast?

METHOD

Preheat the oven to 200°C, 400°F, Gas Mark 6.

Melt the butter and lightly soak each side of the bread sticks.

Mix the sugars and cinnamon together and dip the sticks in the mixture on each side and the ends. Lay the sticks on a baking sheet on baking parchment and bake in the oven for about 8 minutes then remove from the oven, turn the sticks over by one side, return to the oven for another 5 minutes or until golden brown. Allow them to cool a little and crisp up. I enjoy dipping my Cinnamon Bread Sticks into my black coffee.

Sometimes I've believed as many as six impossible things before breakfast.

Lewis Carroll

PORRIDGE (V)

INGREDIENTS

For three to four people:

A 'cup' is about 250 grams or 8 ounces

1 ½ Cups ordinary porridge oats

½ Cup jumbo oats

1 Level teaspoon salt. This is an essential ingredient, even if you do not like the thought of salt in your porridge, you will see how much better it is when you put it in

3 Cups water or 2 cups of water and a cup of milk. (4 cups if you like your porridge sloppy). The addition of milk can make it too creamy and a bit more fattening

A staple in Scotland and it is essential for cold and frosty mornings. It really keeps you warm and is very good for everything in life. You must, however get the right kind of porridge oats. Jumbo oats are good but you lose the creaminess of the porridge. Ordinary, supermarket porridge oats can be a bit floury – no texture. I like to mix ordinary porridge oats with some jumbo oats.

METHOD

Mix all the ingredients together in a saucepan and bring to the boil stirring all the time. Reduce to a light simmer and simmer for five minutes, very slowly, stirring a little every now and then. Serve.

Or, if you have a four-oven Aga, put all the ingredients in a casserole with a lid - you will need 4 cups of water and/or milk – and put into the bottom left oven – the coolest oven – and leave overnight. By the morning you will have a perfect porridge.

I have put in a cup of chopped dried fruit; apricots, prunes, sultanas, sweetened cranberries for example. You need to cook the porridge a little longer and add a little more water if the porridge gets too sticky. You should still add the salt even if you think it might not work. Serve with cream or milk, dark brown soft sugar or honey or maple syrup or a couple of teaspoons of jam. Here in Cornwall, we enjoy a couple of teaspoons of Clotted Cream.

Never work before breakfast. If you have to work before breakfast, get your breakfast first.

Josh Billings (*in total agreement with this ethic – Hugo*)

RICE PORRIDGE (V, GF)

INGREDIENTS

For 4 to 6 people:

100g (4oz) flaked pudding rice or ordinary pudding rice – note the simmering times on the packet might be different

400ml (1 can) coconut milk

400ml – a can full of semi-skimmed ordinary milk

Pinch nutmeg – or a couple of scrapes from a whole nutmeg

2 tablespoon runny honey

An inch knob of fresh ginger, peeled and finely grated

A ripe mango

50g (2oz) flaked almonds, toasted in a hot oven for 5 minutes

A drizzle of honey

A cold rice pudding breakfast, very popular in Asia and India. Some Rice Porridge is savoury and some is just rice and water boiled up for ages producing a very unappetising porridge – but very good glue! This is a Thai adaptation.

METHOD

Put the rice, milk, coconut milk and nutmeg into a pan and bring slowly to a simmer, stirring all the time. Simmer for 8 minutes, stirring quite regularly, allowing the mixture to thicken. If you can't find flaked pudding rice and are using ordinary pudding rice, you will need to simmer for about 25 minutes. If it thickens too much and the rice is still hard, reduce the heat, add a little water or milk and continue stirring until it becomes a thick sauce.

Meanwhile, peel off the skin of a mango, cut in half, running the knife down the flat, round stone in the middle. Cut the flesh into little cubes. (You can do this without peeling but I find it impossible to describe! They do it a lot on television cooking shows, so, watch out for it.) Toast the almonds for about 5 minutes in a hot oven.

Add the honey and the ginger to the porridge stir a few times, taste to see if it is sweet enough for you then remove from the heat, pour into a shallow bowl and allow to cool. Serve warm or cold – nicer, in my view, cold.

Spoon out two or three tablespoons of porridge into a little bowl to serve, add a spoon of mango chunks and almonds. Drizzle some more honey over the top. For different topping; squish out some pomegranate seeds out of a halved pomegranate and some skinned pistachio nuts and sprinkle them over the top of the porridge or; fresh blueberries, roasted crushed pecan nuts and maple syrup (very American).

PORRIDGE BRULEE AND PRUNE COMPOTE (V)

INGREDIENTS

To serve 8 (or 4 Trenchermen):

For Prune Compote:

250g (9oz) pitted prunes

½ small orange, quartered and very thinly sliced

A cinnamon stick

½ litre (17fl oz) apple juice – preferably the cloudy type

For the Porridge Brûlée:

5 egg yolks (use the whites for Egg White Omelette Page 52)

50g (2oz) caster vanilla sugar – sugar that has had a vanilla pod resting in it for ages – or:

A teaspoon vanilla essence – if you don't have vanilla sugar

100ml (4fl oz) hot full fat milk

475ml (16fl oz) double cream or (whipping cream if you prefer a light Brûlée)

35g (1½oz) porridge oats

100g (4oz) golden caster sugar or Demerara sugar

I love this light, slightly stylish, Brunch starter. Who would have thought that such humble ingredients – eggs, prunes, cream, porridge oats – could produce such a wonderful Brunch! It is best prepared the day before and finished off and served the next morning/early afternoon. This is usually our Christmas morning treat.

METHOD

Put the prunes, orange slices and the cinnamon stick into a saucepan and fill with water to just below the surface of the fruit. Bring slowly to the boil; reduce to a simmer for five minutes. Remove from the heat and pour in the apple juice, stir and leave to cool overnight. In the morning, take out the cinnamon stick and serve the compote cold. Put the egg yolks, caster sugar (and vanilla essence, if required) into a large glass mixing bowl. With an electric whisk (or a balloon whisk, if you have the muscles) whisk the eggs and sugar until they turn pale. Gradually add the hot milk, constantly whisking and then pour in the cream and the porridge oats, whisk gently for another 30 seconds and then cover and place in the fridge for at least 8 hours or over-night.

Pre-heat the oven 130°C, 250°F, Gas Mark 1.

Seal one end of 8 chefs' rings (3½ cm deep X 7cm wide rings) with a couple of layers of cling-film to form a cup. Place the cups onto a baking tray. Whisk up the Brûlée mixture, to separate the porridge, and pour equally into the rings. Place into the oven and bake for 45 minutes. Remove from the oven and allow the Brûlées to cool.

To serve; gently remove the cling-film; place the ring onto the centre of a plate, gently peal the cling-film off the bottom of the chef-ring, not lifting the ring too high off the plate – like removing a sticking plaster off a particularly sore wound. Sprinkle some Golden caster sugar over the top; run a clean, small knife around the inside of the ring and gently raise the ring, leaving the Brûlée behind. With a mini-blowtorch, melt the sugar on top. Put a tablespoon of cold compote on the side and serve with pride. You will find the porridge forms a little base to the light custard on top. The thin, crispy layer of sugar just needs a little tap to break into that creamy wonderfulness – I am getting carried away. If you can't find Chefs rings, use ramekins, unfortunately, you will not be able to turn the Brûlées out. I find Chefs' Rings invaluable and use them for a lot of things; from forming fishcakes and potato hash cakes, to help presenting food on the plate.

BREAKFAST SUMMER CRUMBLE (V)

INGREDIENTS

For 4 to 8 people:

50g (2oz) Demerara sugar – the more unrefined, the better

50g (2oz) Plain white flour

50g (2oz) Rolled or jumbo oats (or porridge oats)

40g (1½oz) Very cold butter

500ml (just under a pint) Thick yoghurt full-fat or low fat

A few drops of good vanilla essence

200g (8oz) Mixed summer berries (fresh or frozen). It can be just strawberries and blackcurrants or raspberries and blackberries – or all of them and more! Cooked rhubarb will go well and very good for breakfast

50g (2oz) Ready-to-eat apricots cut into two

2 Dessert spoons maple syrup or honey (optional)

Juice ½ a lemon

150ml (¼ pint) Apple juice

METHOD

These are very good for getting fruit and yoghurt in to a fussy child in the morning.

You will need four 200ml (½ pint) tumbler or 'rocks' glasses (don't use the cut lead-crystal glasses!). If you think the glasses will be too much, you can do this using 8 large ramekins

Pre-heat the oven 200°C, 400°F, gas mark 6.

Put into the food processor with pastry blades – the sugar, flour, oats and the butter in small cubes. Give the mixture a 10 second burst two or three times with the 'pulse' button. If you do not use a food processor, rub the same ingredients, with your finger-tips, in a bowl until the crumble resembles big bread crumbs. Spread the crumble thinly on a thick baking sheet and place in the pre-heated oven for 5 minutes. Remove from the oven and mix the crumble up, spread out evenly again and put back in the oven for another five minutes. Remove and leave to cool. If the crumble is not crumbly enough, pop the tray back in for a couple more minutes.

Put all the fruit into a saucepan with the maple syrup or honey (if you are sweet enough, leave it out), with the lemon juice and the apple juice. Bring to the boil and then reduce to simmer for five minutes. Remove from the heat and leave to cool.

Mix the yoghurt with the vanilla essence. Divide the cooled fruit between the glasses. Pour in the yoghurt equally leaving at least 2cm (¾ inch) gap to the top. Sprinkle the crumble over the top of each. Pat down gently and put into the fridge for at least an hour. The juice of the fruit will mingle with the yoghurt.

COFFEE COMPOTE CRUMBLE (V)

INGREDIENTS

For the Compote:

A total weight of 250g (8oz) of:

Ready-to-eat dried apricots
Dried figs, halved
Pitted prunes
Dried apple rings (halved)
'Golden' or Australian sultanas,
Raisins
Half a lemon, halved and very
thinly sliced
A cinnamon stick
Half litre apple juice – preferably
the cloudy type

For topping:

50g (2oz) Demerara sugar –
the more unrefined, the better
50g (2oz) Plain white flour
Half a teaspoon ground cinnamon
1 teaspoon zest of lemon
50g (2oz) Rolled or Jumbo oats
(or porridge oats)
40g (1 ½) very cold butter
500ml (just under a pint) thick
Yoghurt full-fat or low fat
2 tablespoons of cooled, strong
espresso coffee

We enjoy this in the winter months, don't know why, it just seems a more 'wintery' thing; it is a comforting something to start with.

METHOD

You will need four 200ml (half pint) cappuccino cups. If you think the cups will be too much, you can do this using 8 large ramekins. I have used glasses for you to see the layers.

Pre-heat the oven – 200°C, 400°F, gas mark 6.

Put all the fruit and the cinnamon stick into a saucepan and fill with water to just below the surface of the fruit. Bring slowly to the boil; reduce to a simmer for 10 minutes. Remove from the heat and pour in the apple juice to just above the surface of the fruit, stir in and leave to cool overnight.

Put into the food processor with pastry blades – the sugar, flour, oats, cinnamon, lemon zest and the butter in small cubes. Give the mixture 2 second bursts, two or three times with the 'pulse' button. If you do not use a food processor, rub the same ingredients, with your finger-tips, in a bowl until the crumble resembles big bread crumbs. Spread the crumble thinly on a thick baking sheet and place in the pre-heated oven for 5 minutes. Remove from the oven and mix the crumble up, spread out evenly again and put back in the oven for another five minutes. Remove and leave to cool. If the crumble is not crumbly enough, pop the tray back in for a couple more minutes.

Mix the yoghurt with the coffee. Divide the fruit compote between the cappuccino coffee cups. Pour in the yoghurt equally leaving at least 2cm gap to the top. Sprinkle the crumble over the top of each. Pat down gently and put into the fridge for at least an hour. The juice of the fruit will mingle with the yoghurt.

BREAKFAST FRUIT COMPOTE (V, GF, DF)

INGREDIENTS

For a bowlful to feed about four people for a couple of breakfasts:

A total weight of 250g (8oz) of:

Ready-to-eat dried apricots

Dried figs, halved

Pitted prunes

Dried apple rings, halved

'Golden' or Australian sultanas

Raisins

½ A lemon, halved and very thinly sliced

1 Small orange, quartered and very thinly sliced

A cinnamon stick

½ litre (1 pint) Apple juice – preferably the cloudy type

METHOD

Very good for morning movements – if you get my drift!

Put all the fruit and the cinnamon stick into a saucepan and fill with water to just below the surface of the fruit. Bring slowly to the boil; reduce to a simmer for five minutes. Remove from the heat and pour in the apple juice to just above the surface of the fruit, stir in and leave to cool overnight. In the morning, take out the cinnamon stick and serve the compote cold with some thick, creamy yoghurt.

In the Summer I chop in some fresh pineapple and fresh nectarines after the compote is cooked. The storage time reduces to about two days as opposed to five days, in the fridge.

NB – in one of the better restaurants near Padstow, Cornwall, the chef uses compote instead of treacle in a steamed pudding; it is the best ever pudding! I think there is a little treacle added.

Hope is a good breakfast but a bad supper.

Francis Bacon

SALAD WITH FRUIT (V, GF, DF)

INGREDIENTS

For a generous bowl for 2 people:

For the Fruit:

1 Mango

1 Pomegranate

2 thick slices of fresh pineapple

3 tablespoons of fresh Blueberries

A quarter of a water melon

Black pepper

For the Salad Dressing:

2 tablespoons runny honey or maple syrup (which is not as sweet as honey)

2 tablespoons lemon juice

3 tablespoons cranberry juice

2 tablespoons Raspberry (or strawberry or red wine) vinegar or 1 tablespoon of Balsamic vinegar

As opposed to Fruit Salad, this salad with fruit has an unusual sharp dressing – a real eye-opener. All the fruit have some kind of medicinal property in them, things like anti-carcinogens, stuff that lowers cholesterol, anti oxidants, plus lots of vitamins and fibre.

METHOD

Slice off the flesh from the central stone of the Mango, cut into slices and cut off the skin. Chop the flesh into chunks and put into the mixing bowl. Cut the pomegranate in half and squeeze out the juicy pips into the bowl, or remove them with a little spoon (a ripe pomegranate will be quite juicy so, try and cut it in half over the fruit mixing bowl, without slicing your hand!). Remove any white pith that might escape into the bowl when you scrape out the pips. Slice off the skin and the centre core of the pineapple and chop into chunks and into the mixing bowl. Add the blueberries and the watermelon chunks (with or without pips as you prefer, the pips are quite good for digestion).

Mix all the ingredients together and taste to see if you would prefer it sweeter or sharper. I have also added a couple of grinds of black pepper – believe it or not – this brings out a lot of the sweet flavours. You could add any other fruit like strawberries or Star fruit but I would not use oranges or grapefruit unless you compensate the sharpness with the dressing. I would also avoid bananas, Kiwi fruit and soft fruits as they go into mush nearly instantly.

For the Salad Dressing whisk all the ingredients together in a small bowl. Serve with a little fat-free crème fraiche or yoghurt – it is, however, best and better for you on its own. One feels particularly virtuous after a bowl of this salad.

ORANGE SALAD (V, GF, DF)

INGREDIENTS

2 Oranges

2 Blood oranges or a grapefruit

250ml water

½ a cinnamon stick

2 tablespoons demerara sugar

Small sprig fresh rosemary

Oh, what joy! This is not only my favourite fruity thing in the morning, but possibly the simplest thing to make. It is so simple, I debated whether to include it in this sophisticated recipe book. I decided it is a vital late summer part of breakfast and brunch and should be in these pages.

METHOD

Cut the skin off 2 ordinary and 2 blood oranges or a grapefruit. The art is to run the knife just under the white pith and not take too much of the flesh. A very sharp knife is always good for this job. Don't throw the skins of 2 of the oranges.

In 250ml (just over half a pint) water, put in half a cinnamon stick and 2 tablespoons Demerara sugar (Demerara sugar has a little more character and brings out the orange flavours), a small sprig (about 5 cm – 2 inches) fresh rosemary. Put all these ingredients in a saucepan with the orange peel of 2 of the oranges. Bring the water to the boil and simmer for 5 minutes. Then, allow to cool with the bits in – strain off the bits when the liquid is cool.

Slice the oranges as thinly as possible. Slice them from side to side; not stem to stern, if you see what I mean. This shows off the segments of the orange. Be very careful; for some reason the only time I cut myself – in 35 years of 'cheffing' – is when I slice oranges!! Place the slices neatly in a bowl and pour over the liquor. And that's it – that simple, but very, very popular for Brunch.

If you want to serve this as a refreshing intercourse dish at a dinner party, add some Kirsch or orange liquor.

POACHED PEARS AND JELLY (V, GF)

INGREDIENTS

For 4 to 6 people:

6 large or 8 small pears

350g (12oz) caster sugar

½ a lemon

Pinch of saffron

2 medium size fresh bay leaves

250ml (9fl oz) dry, full white wine

4 sheets gelatine

An Autumn treat. Make the day before. My friend Adrian - chef/proprietor at the famous Padstow Restaurant, Margot's Bistro - helped me with this; he adds saffron to his Poached Pears – a little different and very stylish! Adrian serves this in his restaurant for pudding, which I never have room for. I take it home and have mine for breakfast which is far more enjoyable!

METHOD

Peel the pears leaving the stalks on. Place the pears, the half lemon in a saucepan with a lid. Put in enough water to cover the fruit. Add the rest of the ingredients (not the gelatine). Put on a lid, bring to the boil and then reduce the heat to a simmer for 30 minutes – or when the fruit is soft. This will depend as to how big the pears are and how ripe. Test by putting in a small knife and if the knife slides out with ease, they are ready.

Gently remove the pears and set aside to cool. Try to stand them on their bottoms. Take out the lemon and squeeze out any juice into the liquor. Bring the liquor up to a simmer and reduce by about a third – about 30 minutes. Then stir in 4 sheets of gelatine into 500ml (17 fl.oz.) of the hot liquor. When the gelatine has melted pour the liquid into 4 or 6 small, metal pie moulds about 8cm X 5cm high and, when the liquid has cooled, put the pears and the jelly into the fridge.

To serve; pop the jelly moulds into some hot water for a couple of secs, to loosen the jelly, turn onto a plate, then slice a thin slice off the bottom of the pear to allow it to stand on a plate safely. Serve with some thick yoghurt or crème fraiche or (if in Cornwall) some clotted cream, or simply on its own.

AMERICAN PANCAKES (V)

INGREDIENTS

For 16 pancakes or 4 'Short Stacks'

250g (9oz) Plain flour – sifted

Pinch of salt

1 Teaspoon caster sugar

4 Teaspoons baking powder

2 Beaten eggs, whisked into 300ml (½ pint) milk

30g (1oz) Melted, then cooled a bit, unsalted butter

American pancakes are small, thick and fluffy – just like a Hollywood starlet! You order in 'Stacks' and, in California, it is served with a very sweet, very unpleasant, whisked-up butter-cream, Blueberry Sauce and sugar! However, they also serve them with crispy streaky bacon and maple syrup which I can highly recommend. I have not made these pancakes at all sweet.

METHOD

Mix the flour, sugar, a pinch of salt and baking powder together. Make a well in the middle of the flour, pour in the eggs and milk and, with a wooden spoon gradually stir in the eggs and milk, incorporating the flour from the sides, then, beat the mixture to make a smooth batter. Change to a whisk and whisk in the butter. Leave to stand for an hour – overnight wouldn't matter. Should it thicken overnight, whisk in a couple of tablespoons of milk leaving the batter still quite thick.

The trick of the pancake is to use very little oil. The pan must be hot, heat the oil in it then empty the oil leaving only a very little or brush the oil on with a pastry brush. Put a tablespoon of batter into the pan and flip over when you see bubbles appear on the top of the mixture – after about a minute. Cook for a further minute or so. Cook them just before you sit for breakfast, they don't store very well and you lose the slightly crispy outside and the fluffy inside if you leave them hanging around too long.

BLUEBERRY PANCAKES (V)

These are all the rage at the moment, the theory is Blueberries have anti-oxidants and help prevent cancer. Just drop a punnet (125g/5oz - ish) of fresh or frozen Blueberries into the batter before frying. The berries will pop and the juice will colour the pancakes a deep purple. The Dutch eat their pancakes with melted, unsalted butter and dusting of icing sugar. Also see Blueberry Muffins page 30.

CINNAMON HOTCAKES (V)

INGREDIENTS

For about 20 hotcakes:

200g (7oz) self-raising flour

1 teaspoon ground cinnamon

1 teaspoon baking powder

½ teaspoon bicarbonate of soda

2 large eggs

200ml (7fl oz) low-fat yoghurt

100ml (4fl oz) milk

2 tablespoons maple syrup

Oil for frying

A cross between a pancake, a drop scone and a waffle. This is a great accompaniment with anything including blueberries and ice cream, slice bananas and maple syrup, crispy bacon and scrambled eggs. Or on their own with butter and jam.

METHOD

Sift the flour, cinnamon, baking powder and bicarbonate of soda into a mixing bowl. Into another mixing bowl, whisk all the liquid ingredients together – not the oil. With a hand-whisk running, pour the liquid into the centre of the flour and whisk the liquid ingredients into the flour, drawing the flour into the centre and ensuring the whole lot forms a thick batter.

Heat a non-stick frying pan to quite a high heat. Put in a drop of oil and brush it around the pan. Put in a tablespoon of batter and cook until bubbles form on the top of the cake. Flip over and cook for about 30 to 45 seconds. Cook 2 or 3 hotcakes at a time. Serve as soon as possible. Keep the hotcakes – as their name would imply – warm and serve warm.

You could add fruit in with the batter such as; a couple of tablespoons of Blueberries, or some mashed up, ripe bananas or yellow Australian sultanas. The batter could be made the night before. But it could thicken up so, whisk in a tablespoon or two of milk before cooking.

Eat breakfast like a king, lunch like a prince, and dinner like a pauper.

Adelle Davis

SWEET POTATO PANCAKES (V)

INGREDIENTS

To make 14 to 16 pancakes

250g (9oz) peeled, sweet potato, chopped into small chunks, cooked for about 15 minutes and cooled

3 tablespoons crème fraiche

4 eggs

1 tablespoon caster sugar

½ teaspoon vanilla essence

75g (3oz) self raising flour

1 teaspoon baking powder

Tablespoon melted butter

Vegetable or groundnut oil for frying

Something I thought would go well with the Beetroot Pancake – again sweetish, not savoury and a lovely looking pancake.

METHOD

Whiz up the lot (not the oil for frying) in a food processor into a batter. Allow the mixture to rest for 30 minutes and then heat a little oil and put a tablespoon of the mixture into the pan. Turn after bubbles form on the top and serve in a 'stack' – warm. Try with a dollop of crème fraiche or clotted cream and with raspberry or strawberry sauce or coulis.

BEETROOT PANCAKES (V)

INGREDIENTS

To make 14 to 16 pancakes

250g cooked fresh beetroot, peeled and cooled

3 tablespoons crème fraiche

4 eggs

1 tablespoon caster sugar

A good pinch (½ teaspoon) cinnamon.

100g (4oz) self raising flour

1 teaspoon baking powder

Tablespoon melted butter

Vegetable or groundnut oil for frying

An adapted recipe of an 18th Century, colourful pancake. It was said to be best eaten with game – something eaten regularly for breakfast in the 'old days'. This and the sweet potato pancake don't taste like they sound (if you know what I mean). They go with both sweet and savoury dishes or can be served on their own.

METHOD

Whiz up the lot (not the oil for frying) in a food processor into a batter. Allow the mixture to rest for 30 minutes and then heat a little oil and put a tablespoon of the mixture into the pan. Turn after bubbles form on the top (they cook and burn quite quickly) and serve in a 'stack' warm or cold, with sweet or savoury dishes.

AMERICAN BLUEBERRY OR RASPBERRY MUFFINS (V)

INGREDIENTS

For 24 small or 12 large Muffins:

110g (4oz) Very soft unsalted butter

170g (6oz) Caster sugar

½ Teaspoon vanilla extract or the scraped out seeds of a vanilla pod

1 Pinch salt

2 Large beaten eggs

250ml (½ pint) Milk

2 Teaspoons baking powder

340g (12oz) Self-raising flour

10g (¼ oz) Ground almonds

150g (6oz) Punnet fresh or frozen raspberries or blueberries

Not to be confused with 'English Muffins' which are round bread rolls similar to Crumpets. I really like little Muffins, they are bite-size and won't fill you up if you want to have a huge breakfast. A large, regular Muffin seems to fill me up. They have to be baked and eaten on the same morning; however, the dough lasts up to 3 days in the fridge.

METHOD

Pre-heat oven at 180°C, 350°F, gas mark 4.

Beat together the butter, sugar, vanilla essence and salt until the mixture is quite pale, nearly white and fluffy. An electric hand-whisk is best for this. Slowly whisk in the beaten egg a bit at a time to prevent splitting. Sieve the flour and baking powder and then fold into the butter mix, gently with a wooden spoon, then fold in the ground almonds. Add, gradually, the milk so that the mixture is the consistency of wet bread-dough – or as Stewart, a patisserie chef friend of mine (and major contributor to this recipe) says; "until the mixture is reluctant to fall from the spoon" – you don't necessarily need all the milk.

Place a little mixture in the base of each muffin mould. Put in a raspberry or a couple of blueberries and then cover up to just below the lip of the mould, with more mixture. You will need to put in more raspberries or blueberries in the larger moulds. Push in a raspberry or blueberry on the top of the mix.

Bake in the pre-heated oven for 12 to 15 minutes. When you remove the muffins from the oven you might feel they are not cooked enough. They are best eaten warm and slightly soggy inside. They can be, however, a bit of a devil to get out of the moulds. Allow them to cool a little before you turn them out onto a cooling rack.

AMERICAN BLUEBERRY SCONES (V)

INGREDIENTS

For 6 scones:

275g (10oz) Plain flour

1 tablespoon baking powder

50g (2oz) Granulated sugar

½ teaspoon salt

2 teaspoons grated zest of lemon

75g (3oz) cold unsalted butter cut into little 1cm pieces

175g (6oz) fresh Blueberries (although I have used dried when I can't find fresh but it is not as good)

175ml (6fl oz) double cream

4 tablespoons icing sugar

2 teaspoons lemon juice

These are sometimes called biscuits in the States. In Massachusetts, America, my sister-in-law has a wonderful B&B or Inn, as it is called there, called 'Amscot'. It is in a very old (in American terms) house, built in 1734 and it full of New England character. This recipe is one of the many delicious things sister-in-law, Viki, offers her guests in the morning. I suppose you could serve these for Tea but they are a little different to English Tea scones. These scones have to be eaten the morning they are cooked. They will go so make plenty.

METHOD

Pre-heat the oven to 220°C, 425°F, gas mark 7.

Put the dry ingredient – including the lemon zest - into a mixing bowl or a food processer with the pastry blades. Rub or mix in the cold butter, or cut the butter in with a knife until it resembles coarse breadcrumbs. Avoid handling as much as possible, you should keep the pastry cool, place into the fridge for at least 30 minutes before the next stage. You could do this the night before.

If you have used the food processer turn the mixture into a mixing bowl and stir in blueberries using a spoon, and then the cream to bring the dough together and divide into two, form each lump into a ball. Place the balls onto a floured surface. Sprinkle with flour and pat each ball down to about 2 centimetres (½ inch) thick and 10 to 13cm (4 to 5 inches) in diameter. Cut the 'cakes' into 6 wedges each and place each wedge, spaced well, on a baking sheet covered in baking parchment. Bake for 12 to 14 minutes.

Meanwhile make the icing: Mix the icing sugar with the lemon juice to produce a thick pouring consistency. Take the scones out of the oven and allow them to cool slightly on a wire rack. Put a generous dollop of icing on each scone and serve slightly warm. You will find they will go within seconds so keep one back for you!

BANANA BREAD (V)

INGREDIENTS

100g sultanas

1 Earl Grey tea bag

3 large or 4 small bananas

75g (3oz) soft butter

200g (8oz) granulated sugar

1 large egg

1 teaspoon vanilla essence

1 teaspoon baking soda

A pinch of salt

200g (8oz) plain flour

Just the best way to use up old bananas. I also found that my local big supermarket was flogging off over-ripe bananas cheaply. You will – I can assure you – be making tons of this bread! It is more of a cake than bread as it is not made with yeast. Very good on picnics. I like to do this in a food processor, but if you like a lumpy, rustic effect, use a large bowl and a wooden spoon to mix everything up with a lot of elbow power.

METHOD

Pre-heat oven 190°C, 375°F, gas mark 5.

Make up a small cup of Earl Grey tea and soak the sultanas for at least 6 hours – overnight would be better. The sultanas will become lovely and plump.

In a food processor with the double blades, or the plastic dough blades, put in the rest of the ingredients (not the flour). Mix all the ingredients together in the processor until you have a smooth batter and then add the flour (except a dessert spoonful) a spoon at a time whilst the machine is running.

Drain the tea from the sultanas, mix in the withheld spoon of flour to cover the sultanas (this stops them sinking to the bottom of the loaf) and then fold in the lovely plump sultanas into the batter.

Butter a 100cm x 200cm (5" x 8") loaf tin, cut out some baking parchment to fit the bottom of the tin and pour in the batter mix. Put in the centre of the oven and bake for 60 minutes. Check after 45 minutes to see if the top is brown enough – if it is, finish off the baking with some foil to stop the top burning.

Turn out, peel off the baking parchment and cool the loaf on a cooling rack.

MADELEINES (V)

INGREDIENTS

For 10 to 12 Madeleines:

1 Large egg

2 Drops of vanilla essence

50g (2oz) Granulated sugar

50g (2oz) Sifted plain flour

50g (2oz) Very soft unsalted butter (not quite melted)

The grated rind of a small orange

A tablespoon of orange water

Icing sugar

Very French, Madeleines are served with a bowl of very strong coffee. They are a light cake/biscuit with a hint of orange. They should be baked in a special scalloped baking tray but you could use a mince pie baking tray. This is sometimes the only thing a Parisian has for breakfast – possibly why they are all so thin!

METHOD

Pre-heat oven at 190°C, 375°F, gas mark 5.

Whisk the egg, vanilla essence and sugar in a bowl to a 'soft peak' consistency – where you leave a peak in the mix when you take out the whisk. Sift the flour over the mixture and fold gently with a spatula, then fold in the very soft butter and the grated orange zest. Leave for at least an hour in the fridge. Fill each Madeleine mould or tart mould level to the top and bake for 8 minutes. When baked, turn the cakes out onto a cooling rack and dust with icing sugar. Serve cool with hot, strong coffee or thick, dark hot chocolate (page 114).

All happiness depends on a leisurely breakfast.

John Gunther

NECTARINE DANISH PASTRY (V)

INGREDIENTS

To make 6 pastries:

375g pack of puff pastry, preferable ready rolled

3 to 4 ripe nectarines, depending on size

25g (1oz) butter

Juice of ½ a lemon

55g (2oz) Demerara sugar

1 teaspoon vanilla extract

2 teaspoons cornflour mixed with 2 tablespoons cold water

25g (1oz) melted butter

For the frosting:

4 tablespoons icing sugar

1 teaspoon lemon juice

Water

This is for those Europeans who have very small, fluffy-pastry-type breakfasts and brunch. These freeze well un-cooked or baked, so you can make a whole batch and produce them when you want. You can have them with or without frosting (best with, in my view). I like to dollop the frosting on with a spoon so it looks home made. I like everybody to see that I haven't gone out to the local supermarket and picked up the usual Danish pastry. Anyway; what supermarket or baker is going to serve Nectarine Danishes?!!

METHOD

Roll out the pastry to 1/2cm thick and 35cm X 22.5cm (13 ¾ X 9 inches). Then cut into 6 equal squares 12 X 12 cm (4 ¾ inches). Remember, if you need to re-roll the pastry again, just fold the bits together so that it keeps the puffy layers in the pastry – don't munge it all up like you would a dough or short-crust pastry. Keep the squares chilled in the fridge whilst you make the filling. For the filling, halve then stone the nectarines. Slice each half into 6 to 8 slices. Melt the butter, lemon juice and sugar in a wide-based saucepan and allow the sugar to melt, stirring all the time over a gentle heat. Add the nectarines and the vanilla extract and toss gently in the butter and remove from the heat.

Pre-heat the oven to 230°C, 450°F, gas mark 8.

Take each pastry square and place onto a baking sheet lined with baking parchment. Twist one corner one way a full twist, the opposite corner a full twist the other way. Lift out 6 or 8 slices of nectarine with a fork, leaving the juice in the pan, and arrange in a neat row from twisted corner to the other twisted corner. Fold the non-twisted corners over the top of the filling, pinch together and twist to seal. Repeat this with the other five pastries. Warm up the juice in the pan and stir in the cornflour and water mixture. This will thicken the sauce. When the sauce is nice and thick and cooked through, spoon a couple of teaspoons onto the exposed fruit on each pastry. When you have made all the pastries, put them into a fridge to cool for an hour. Meanwhile, make the frosting. Just mix the ingredients together into a smooth paste. It should be nearly as thick as runny toothpaste. Add water or more sugar to get it to the right consistency. Keep at room temperature.

Bake the pastries for 15 to 20 minutes. When they are golden brown, take them out and place on a cooling rack. Brush each pastry with melted butter. Spoon the frosting over the Danishes whilst they are hot and serve when they have cooled a bit but are still warm. If you are adept enough; make a cone out of greaseproof paper, fill it with frosting, snip off the end and pipe the frosting in little lines over the top of the Danish. They won't, however, look very home made! Do this on a cooling rack (with a bit of paper underneath to catch the spills). If you are freezing the pastries, don't put on the frosting. You can bake the cooked ones from frozen: about 15min in oven 180°C, 350°F, gas mark 4.

BANANA FOSTER (V, GF)

INGREDIENTS

For 4 people;

50g (2oz) Unsalted butter

175g (7oz) Soft brown sugar

½ Teaspoon cinnamon

60ml (2fl oz) Banana liqueur

4 Bananas

60ml (2fl oz) Dark rum

Known in America, as one of the best breakfasts for the-morning-after-the-night-before. I had this breakfast in Bermuda (not, I hasten to add, because of over indulgence) and it was a wonderful change to the norm. It is, somehow, more of a breakfast than a 'pudding'.

METHOD

Melt in a large frying pan; unsalted butter, soft brown sugar, cinnamon and melt over a low heat, stirring all the time.

Next; stir in the banana liqueur – Crème de Banane for example (there is always some in the bottom of the liqueur cabinet that someone gave you and has never been touched!) then 4 bananas cut lengthways in half.

Fry everything until going a deep brown. Stir but don't break up the bananas. Bring up the heat and add the dark rum.

Bring to the boil and set light to the rum (flambé) and serve with some thick double cream or vanilla ice cream.

A bachelor's life is a fine breakfast, a flat lunch, and a miserable dinner.

Francis Bacon

EGGS INTRO

I think 'La Delia' has done eggs – how to fry, boil and poach and eat an egg. Breakfast eggs must be as fresh as possible, free-range and/or organic. They should be stored in their box; pointed end down and left in a cool, shaded place – not in a fridge. In the summer the whites can seem a little watery; this is because the free range hens are drinking more when they get hot. In the summer I use 'Barn Eggs' for poaching and frying.

Poaching can be done quite simply by putting boiled water (some people put in a drop of vinegar in the water) into a small pan – a non-stick frying pan is even better – with a lid. Break an egg into a cup (to make sure the yolk is intact), pour the egg gently into the water just as it turns into a simmer, reducing the heat and poach for about 4 minutes. This method will mean you can do two to four eggs at a time. The egg will look like a fried egg without the brown bits. To achieve a kind of traditional, spherical poached egg you need to whisk up nearly-boiling water into a whirlpool and drop the egg in the middle. This only works if the egg is fresh and the water is in a saucepan. Delia suggests the egg is lifted out with a slotted spoon and placed on a wad of kitchen paper – very good idea but if too dry, the egg sticks to the spoon! Caterers pre-cook lots of poached eggs this way and then plunge them into iced water to stop the cooking. When the poached egg is wanted, put the egg into boiling water for 30 seconds and then serve.

The art of cooking a good egg is not to cook it too hot, the fat should not be hot for frying, the water should not be at a rolling boil for poaching and scrambled egg should be done on a gentle heat, stirring the eggs constantly in a thick bottom pan, with a knob of butter, until creamy scrambled egg is achieved. A friend of mine takes 20 minutes to make his scrambled eggs – a bit extreme but a very good result. If you like creamy scrambled egg but must have the eggs well cooked (if you are pregnant for example), stir in some double cream at the last minute; here in Cornwall, we stir in clotted cream which is pure wickedness. Try not to add pepper as this makes the eggs turn grey and leave out salt as there is enough in the butter. If you like very hard scrambled eggs, you might as well have an omelette!

Boiled eggs with soldiers are an old favourite; don't forget to stick a pin in the fat end of the egg to stop it cracking when you lower it into the boiling water. Reduce the water to a simmer for 4 minutes for soft, 6 minutes for hardish, 8 minutes for rock hard, (duck eggs are a couple of minutes more – this is because there is less white and more yolk). If the eggs are very fresh, (a day or two old) you need to add an extra 30 seconds. An RAC hotel inspector we know, puts Marmite on his soldiers. An eccentric friend of mine, who lives in a long-boat, puts Gentleman's Relish on his fingers of toast! My son drops Tabasco onto the yolk before plunging in his soldiers and I have a strange ritual of putting on a little pepper and a sprinkle of celery salt on buttered, toasted crust of bread, before dipping the ensemble into my egg. My wife can't bear to watch my performance with a boiled egg! Don't forget to crush the empty shell so that wicked witches can't crawl in!!!

Crushed Eggs are a wonderful alternative to scrambled, little children enjoy them too: Put a couple of eggs into tepid water, bring to the boil and boil for 6 minutes. As soon as 6 minutes is up, plunge the eggs into cold running water for two minutes. This will allow the shell to be cold enough to peel. Gently peel the eggs – be careful you don't break the white, the yolks are still soft. Put the peeled eggs on thick buttered toast and crush them with the back of a fork. The yolk will ooze over the toast. Serve with a couple of fresh anchovy fillets crossed over the top of the egg and a sprinkle of ground black pepper.

Omelettes are usually reserved for a snack supper except for Omelette Arnold Bennett (page 51) or Rumble-Tumble Omelette (page 50).

The yellowness of eggs has become, for some reason, a test as to their freshness and a mark that they are free-range and/ or organic. The depth of yellow in an egg is produced by either free-range hens eating green food like grass and cabbage leaves, or cornmeal. Nowadays, supermarket eggs (possibly I should say 'some' supermarket eggs) are all a deep yellow in the pretence that they are free-range, when, in fact, they just put a yellow additive in the hen's feed. So, organic is best, the yolks are not necessarily very yellow and the nutritional value is the same, however yellow the yolk is!

Fresh Eggs are tested by putting an egg in a bowl of cold water; if it sinks to the bottom and lies on its side it is fresh. If it stands up it is quite fresh (good for baking and meringues). If an egg floats to the top, it is not fresh and possibly bad.

EGGS BENEDICT

INGREDIENTS

Hollandaise sauce: a sauce blender or hand electric whisk is vital for this sauce

100g (4oz) Clarified butter – melt un-salted butter extremely gently until the milky solids form in the bottom of the pan and you can pour off clear melted butter

1 Tablespoon each of water, and white wine vinegar. Boil both until reduced to one tablespoon

1 Egg yolk

Salt and pepper

4 to 6 Rashers of smoked streaky bacon - rind off. Or some good smoked ham if you want to be traditional

Oil to cook the bacon

1 English muffin – or two slices thick white toast or the crusts, cut into a round about 10cm (4 inches) in diameter

2 Large (very fresh) eggs

A couple of pinches of Cayenne pepper - or crushed red peppercorns

A very international breakfast. I once had Eggs Benedict for breakfast at a very old fashioned gentleman's club in St. James Square in London and thought it the most divine breakfast. I would recommend you have Eggs Benedict for a late Sunday breakfast, with a Bloody Mary (page 43). Traditionally, Eggs Benedict is served with smoked ham, I prefer smoked bacon, it is more breakfasty.

METHOD

First make the Hollandaise sauce: Put into a cold bowl; a tablespoon of the reduced water and vinegar, the egg yolk, salt and pepper, put the bowl over simmering water (don't let the water touch the bowl), with a hand-whisk (electric is best), whisk the egg mixture to a 'Ribbon' consistency – where you can see ribbons when you lift up the whisk – this will take about 5 minutes of continuous whisking! Whilst whisking, gradually add the warm clarified butter. Make sure the water in the pan is at a slow simmer and whisk until the sauce is like very thick cream or a light mayonnaise. Keep warm in a bowl over some hot – not boiling, water in a saucepan.

Brush each side of the bacon with oil, place the rashers under the grill on a sheet of tin foil (it makes grilling less messy) and grill until crispy or nearly crispy. Boil some water with a teaspoon or two of vinegar, in a small, shallow, non-stick saucepan or frying pan with a lid or plate to cover, or use a deep saucepan with lots of water. Crack the eggs into ramekins or teacups. Reduce the water to a slow simmer; pour in the eggs from the teacups gently into the water. Soft poach the eggs for 3 minutes. Meanwhile, cut the muffins in half and toast in the grill. If you are fortunate to have an Aga, put the muffins in the hob-toaster for a minute either side.

Now build your Benedict; you need to be swift to make sure it's hot. Put out two hot medium plates: Put 2 or 3 cooked rashers of bacon, in a cross or a star, on each half of toasted muffin (half on each plate), and pour any oil and juices from the grill pan over the rashers. Take the poached eggs out of the water with a slotted spatula or spoon one at a time, have a wad of kitchen paper ready on which you pat the slotted spoon and the egg to make sure all the water is off, (a 'Delia' trick!) lay the egg on top of the bacon. Spoon enough Hollandaise sauce over the eggs to cover (about a tablespoon or two). Dust the top with a pinch of Cayenne pepper and serve with a grilled tomato with chopped chives on top. Serve with a handful of dressed watercress salad for Sunday Brunch.

EGGS HUSSARDE

INGREDIENTS

For 4 people:

2 English muffin sliced in half

4 slices of good un-smoked, air-dried ham

4 eggs

4 tablespoons Hollandaise sauce (see page 38)

4 tablespoons 'Marchand de Vin Sauce' (see below)

For 'Marchand de Vin' Sauce:

100g (4oz) butter. This may sound a little rich but it is authentic. You could use 6 tablespoons of extra virgin olive oil if you feel the arteries clogging up!

100g (4oz) onion

2 cloves crushed garlic

50g (2oz) – about 4 spring onions, remove the root – use the green bits as well

The best way, I find, is to put these last 3 ingredients into a food processor and to finely chop or mince

75g (3oz) brown mushrooms - minced

50g (2oz) un-smoked ham - minced

40g (1¾oz) plain flour

2 tablespoons Worcestershire sauce

400ml (13fl oz) beef stock

100ml (4fl oz) red wine

2 teaspoons dried thyme

1 bay leaf

3 tablespoons chopped fresh flat leaf parsley

Salt and pepper

This is a New Orleans version of Eggs Benedict, made famous at Brennan's Restaurant in New Orleans. The breakfast menu there is a vision of various eggs, placed on lots of different things like artichoke hearts or flaky pastry and all – it seems – covered in Hollandaise sauce or cheese! This dish has a lovely sauce called 'Marchand de Vin Sauce' - echoes of New Orleans' French origins. I have based the recipe on the one from Brennan's restaurant. I have had to adapt it, quite a bit, to British tastes and measurements. This is one of my favourite Brunches.

METHOD

Melt the butter in a large saucepan over a medium heat. Fry the onion, garlic, and spring onions, for 5 minutes, stirring all the time. Add the minced mushrooms and ham; stir for another 3 minutes over a lower heat. Gradually sprinkle in the flour stirring all the time for another 4 minutes, then stir in the Worcester Sauce, wine, beef stock, thyme and bay leaf – simmer the sauce for at least an hour. Just before serving, add the chopped parsley and the seasoning. Take out the Bay leaf.

For Hollandaise sauce: a sauce blender or hand electric whisk is vital for this sauce. 250g (8oz) clarified butter – melt un-salted butter extremely gently until the milky solids form in the bottom of the pan and you can pour off clear melted butter. 2 tablespoons white wine vinegar. Boil until reduced to one tablespoon, 1 tablespoon water, 1 yolk of egg, salt and pepper.

Put into a cold bowl; a tablespoon of the reduced vinegar and add a tablespoon water, the egg yolk, salt and pepper, put the bowl over simmering water (don't let the water touch the bowel), with a hand-whisk (electric hand-whisk would be better), whisk the egg mixture to a frothy, creamy consistency – this will take about 5 minute of continuous whisking! Now, whilst continuing whisking, gradually add the warm clarified butter. Make sure the water in the pan is at a slow simmer and whisk until the sauce is like thick cream or a light mayonnaise. Keep warm in a bowl over some hot – not boiling, water in a saucepan.

For the rest of the dish: Poach four soft eggs. Warm up the slices of ham. Cut the English Muffin half and toast. If you are fortunate to have an Aga, toast the muffins in the hob-toaster. Once you have everything prepared, you are ready to serve up the Eggs Hussardes: On two hot plates, place half a toasted muffin on each plate and cover with slices of the warm ham. Spoon on about a dessertspoon of the hot Marchand de Vin Sauce - not a huge spoonful, just enough to cover the ham, then put on a poached egg and cover with about a tablespoon of Hollandaise sauce. Serve.

At Brennan's Restaurant you get 2 Eggs Hussardes per person! served, not on English Muffins but on something called a 'Holland Rusk' – not dissimilar to what we gave our children to teeth on in the old days.

COUNTRY DUCK EGG

INGREDIENTS

For each person:

A duck egg

A tablespoon flour, seasoned with plenty of pepper and salt

A chicken egg whisked up

2 tablespoons Panko (Japanese breadcrumbs) or ordinary white breadcrumbs

3 slices of good Black pudding

100g (4oz) spinach

Vegetable oil for deep frying

I was going to call this 'Fried Poached Duck Egg' but I thought it would confuse people – it certainly confused me! This is a lovely egg dish I found in a very old Breakfast book. I have put a modern edge to it and I just love this for breakfast. I have served the 'Country Egg' with black pudding and spinach. Duck eggs have lovely big yolks surrounded by a little white, rich flavour and lot bigger than a hens egg.

METHOD

Firstly, put some ice cubes into a bowl of cold water – at least a pint of water.

Break the duck egg into a teacup or ramekin. Bring some water to boil in a wide pan or a deep frying pan. Add a couple teaspoons vinegar and a teaspoon salt into the water. Reduce the water to a simmer and gently plop in the duck egg and poach for 3 minutes. As soon as it is poached, take out the egg with a slotted spoon and then place the poached egg into the iced water to halt the cooking.

Cook the spinach by putting the washed spinach in a wok or a large frying pan with a knob of butter. Bring to a high heat and throw in the spinach, the spinach will cook with the water on the leaves from washing and the butter. It is cooked when it wilts, drain well and keep it warn. Just before serving, put out a dish of the flour, the whisked egg and the Panko, heat the oil for deep frying (it does not need to be too deep, just deep enough to fry the duck egg). Also put on a frying pan, with a little oil for the black pudding. Whilst the oil is heating, fry the slices of black pudding for a minute on each side over a medium heat. Place the slices of black pudding on the spinach and keep warm.

Take out the chilled poached duck, roll the egg in the seasoned flour, then the whisked egg and finally coat with the Panko breadcrumbs and deep fry for about 1 to 2 minutes, until crispy brown. Any longer will cook the yolk too hard. Take out of the oil with a slatted spoon and place on a wad of kitchen paper to drain the oil and then perch on top of the black pudding, and serve.

CORNISH EGGS (V)

INGREDIENTS

For two people:

Softened butter for spreading

1 English muffin sliced in half

1 heaped tablespoon grated Swiss cheese

2 eggs – separated (don't break the yolk)

1 tablespoon chopped parsley

1 tablespoon chopped chives

1 tablespoon chopped fennel or dill

Salt and freshly ground black pepper

This is a breakfast I found in a New England B&B Cookbook whilst staying in an Inn in Massachusetts. It is lovely, light and original. Why it is call 'Cornish' Baked Eggs, I have no idea, other than a 'Cornish Hen' in America is a small chicken like a Poussin – but this recipe uses regular eggs. This recipe is a house breakfast speciality from 'Inn Britannia', a B&B in Searsport, Maine, USA. This is one of two recipes I have found in an American B&B Cookbook (the other on page 57). I always thought American Breakfasts were either eggs bacon or ham covered in melted cheese, Hollandaise Sauce or hot chilli tomato sauce. I must admit, they do quite a lot of other stuff and what they do cover with melted cheese, Hollandaise Sauce or hot chilli tomato sauce; is delicious!

METHOD

Preheat the oven to 180°C, 350°F, Gas Mark 4.

Butter the English muffin and sprinkle with half of the grated Swiss cheese. Put the muffins onto a baking tray, leave a good space between them. Whisk up the egg whites in a glass bowl until stiff – to a 'peak' as though you were making meringues. Gently fold in the chopped herbs and equally mound the whites onto the muffins. Pop the egg yolk onto the top of each egg white mound and push the yolk into the whites to hold it in place. Sprinkle the rest of the cheese over the top with a little salt and black pepper. Bake for 10 to 14 minutes and serve immediately.

EGGS SEBASTIAN

INGREDIENTS

For 8 scallops (8 or 4 portions, depending on appetite)

For the Sauce Cordelloise:

150ml (5fl oz) ordinary olive oil

A couple of slivers – with a potato peeler - lemon zest; about an eighth of a lemon

1 egg yolk

½ tablespoon lemon juice

1 tablespoon water

A little salt and white pepper

For the finished dish:

A knob of butter and a little oil

8 thick slices of black pudding, keep the skin on. We in Cornwall use 'Hogs Pudden'

8 large scallops, in their half shell. Remove the scallop from the shell with a sharp knife. I like to keep the orange 'corral' attached – Americans throw them away for some reason

Salt and pepper

10 quail's eggs (you are guaranteed to make a mess of at least two of them!)

Quails eggs on seared scallops on black pudding served with a Sauce Cordelloise (olive oil Hollandaise). This is one of the poshest of Brunches. It is not a very big Brunch, it's but a mouthful, so can be eaten by people with a tiny morning appetite. It will impress and delight the palate. This is what I give to 'food snobs' who think breakfast and Brunch are secondary meals. I pretend that we eat this all the time, every day of the week!

METHOD

Pour the olive oil into a small saucepan, with the lemon zest, and bring it up to blood temperature. Let it stand at that temperature for at least half an hour so that the lemon zest infuses into the oil. Meanwhile, put the egg yolk, lemon juice and water, with a little seasoning into a glass bowl. Put the bowl over simmering water (don't let the water touch the bowl), with a hand-whisk (electric hand-whisk would be better), whisk the egg mixture to a light creamy consistency and quite fluffy – this will take about 5 minute of continuous whisking! Remove the bowl and saucepan from the heat. Remove the lemon zest from the oil. Now, whilst continuing whisking, gradually add the warm olive oil. Pour in the oil very, very slowly – a mere dribble. Whisk until the sauce is like very thick cream or a light mayonnaise. Unlike a mayonnaise, if this splits, it is impossible to get back! Keep warm by putting a cloth over it, but don't keep it in the oven.

Now for the finished dish – this all happens quite rapidly. Heat up two frying pans – one on a medium heat, one a little hotter but not 'smoking' hot. Line up the plates and the half scallop shells on the plate. In the hotter pan, put in a knob of butter and a little oil to stop the butter from burning. Put in the slices of black pudding or Hogs Pudden. Fry for a minute each side, remove and place on each scallop shell. Now break eight little quail's eggs into the medium hot pan: I do this by gently cutting the shell of the egg with a serrated knife and cracking them into little cups, then pouring them into the pan. At the same time, pour in a little more butter and oil into the hotter pan (the black pudding pan) and put in the scallops. Season them with a little salt and pepper. Fry for no more than 40 seconds on each side, pressing each one, for a second or two, onto the pan. Put a scallop on each black pudding, the egg on the scallop and 'knap' – or lightly coat – each little stack with the Cordelloise sauce. Dust with a little freshly ground pepper and serve. Serve with some walnut-bread toast and orange juice; it is a great combination and very complementary.

MUMBLES EGGS

INGREDIENTS

You will need:

English Muffins

Eggs

Butter

Gentleman's Relish

Cayenne Pepper or Crushed Red Peppercorns

Tomato

An eighteenth Century breakfast named after the Mumbles Hills. I remember it being served to my father in a very old London hotel, when I was quite small after we had been to see the Royal Tournament. As a child I found it inedible – now I am addicted to this breakfast.

METHOD

For each person make some creamy scrambled egg using 2 eggs. Toast an English Muffin that has been sliced in half and spread on some butter so it melts. Spread on one slice some Gentleman's Relish so that the relish mixes with the melted butter. Spoon the egg on top of the relish, dust a little Cayenne pepper or crushed red peppercorns over the eggs and serve with a baked tomato (a tomato halved and put into a hot oven for about 5 minutes) and a couple of fresh sage leaves for decoration. Perch the other half of the muffin on the side of the eggs.

Gentleman's Relish is a delicious spiced, anchovy paste, a deep greeny-grey in colour. It is quite salty so don't season the scrambled egg. A popular make of Gentleman's Relish is Patum Peperium. Use sparingly as it is quite a concentrated flavour. An acquired taste – but it does not take long to acquire one and when you do, you are addicted!

I'm not the kind of actor that would know what my character had for breakfast last Tuesday.

Liam Neeson

TRAITORS EGGS

INGREDIENTS

You will need:

Blinis (page 66) or Scots Pancakes

Smoked Salmon

Eggs

Milk

Butter or Olive oil

Crème Fraiche or Double Cream

Capers

Fresh Chives

METHOD

My family serves Traitor's Eggs on Good Friday – the traitor referred being Judas Iscariot. This is a variation on a now, very popular hotel and B&B breakfast; smoked salmon and scrambled eggs. It is an art to making good, creamy scramble eggs; slowly and with care. I have known some extraordinary people that make scrambled eggs in a microwave. I am sure it is not good for people; it certainly isn't for the eggs, they turn into a kind of watery cardboard tasting jelly, similar to junket (if you can remember that awful pudding)!

For each person; you need 3 Blinis (see page 66) or Scots pancakes. Chop up a slice (about 15g) of smoked salmon into ribbons – quite narrow ribbons. Make creamy scrambled egg using 2 eggs whisked up with a drop of milk but no seasoning – there is salt in the butter and pepper will turn the eggs grey; melt a little butter or olive oil in a thick-bottom saucepan and stir in the eggs. I like to take at least 5 minutes to gently scramble the eggs over a low heat; keep stirring. As the eggs become a little scrambled – just beyond raw – stir in a good tablespoon of Crème Fraiche or thick double cream (we use clotted cream in Cornwall), then mix into the scrambled eggs a heaped teaspoon of drained capers, and cook very gently for a minute or two more, until the eggs firm up, but still quite creamy, then; in the last 30 seconds, fold in the smoked salmon. Stir in the salmon only a couple of times then serve beside the warmed Blinis or pancakes. Lay a couple of strips of smoked salmon over the top of the egg for extra colour, then sprinkle some fresh chopped chives over the top and serve.

A glass of sparkling Italian wine mixed with Peach Juice – made famous by Harry's Bar in Venice, known as a Bellini – it is a perfect accompaniment with this.

BACON AND MARMALADE SANDWICH

INGREDIENTS

Per person:

2 Thick slices of white bread

Butter

Thick cut marmalade

3-4 rashers lightly smoked or unsmoked bacon

I know; I know – it sounds bizarre but a friend, David McWilliam (designer of 'Bin on the Lash' page 107), has this eccentric attitude to breakfast that seems to work! I will have to admit, this is lovely and very good for a breakfast 'on the hoof' or a desk breakfast. And it is as simple as it sounds...

METHOD

Butter two thick slices of white bread and slather thick-cut marmalade over one slice. Fry lightly smoked or un-smoked back bacon about 3 to 4 rashers per sandwich. Place the bacon on the marmalade whilst hot and sandwich with the other buttered slice. The bacon must be hot when you put it into the sandwich, this melts the butter and the marmalade mingles into the bacon and the bread – simply divine! I tried this sandwich toasted, which is lovely if you are going to eat it as soon as you have toasted it, but the toast will go flobby after only a few minutes if you wrap it up to take to work. Other versions; put the bacon and marmalade in an English muffin or a bun, wholemeal bread is OK but it can dampen the flavour of the contents.

The main reason I get up in the morning is not prayer or meditation, but for breakfast.

Dalai Lama

EGGS MIMOSA

INGREDIENTS

For 2 people:

3 tablespoons softened unsalted* butter

Two thick slices white bread

4 large free range eggs - as fresh as possible

1 small pot Salmon caviar or Saviar – or the real thing - Caviar!

A tablespoon double cream

4 thin slices of Pancetta or very thinly sliced smoked streaky bacon

1 teaspoon crushed black peppercorns

I don't know where this originates from (someone might tell me and I will pass it on). This is a summer, warm morning breakfast for someone you want to impress - a new wife (husband) or the boss and/or a new partner when they stay the night. Fish and eggs always go together so well for Brunch:

METHOD

Pre-heat the oven to 230°C, 450°F, gas mark 8.

Nearly melt 2 tablespoons of the unsalted butter. Cut the bread into two 12 to 15cm discs (about 5 to 6 inches) using a pastry cutter or a teacup and a sharp knife. Paint both sides of the bread disc with the butter and place on a baking sheet. Put into a hot oven for about 6 minutes or until the bread is turning brown and quite crispy. Put a disc on each plate for serving. Heat up a frying pan to a high heat, pour in a teaspoon or two of vegetable oil and then the slices of Pancetta. Fry until quite crisp, keep warm.

Lightly scramble the eggs – melt the third tablespoon of butter in a non-stick pan. Whisk the eggs and stir into the saucepan, continue to stir the egg over a low heat until it becomes lightly scrambled, still creamy, add the cream and continue until just firm. Spoon the scrambled egg equally on each piece of bread, flatten the top of each mound with the back of a spoon. Spoon on the Saviar (or Caviar), a little mound in the middle of the scrambled egg. Crush the pepper corns with a heavy kitchen knife or a mortise and pestle and then sprinkle over the caviar, place two or three rashers of crisp Pancetta on the side.

You could also serve on Blinis (page 66). A glass of Bucks Fizz (the Americans call it Mimosa – possibly hence the name) or a Peach and Mint Fizz (page 112).

*NB My old dad, who used to be a dairy farmer, told me; unsalted butter is not ordinary butter without salt, it is a butter that has a slightly different churning and production process. It has a distinctively, different taste and is eaten more in southern Europe, not so much in the UK. Personally I do not care for it at breakfast with my toasted soldiers, as seems to be the growing trend in the smarter B&B establishments!

HUEVOS RANCHEROS (RANCHER'S EGGS) (V)

INGREDIENTS

For 2 ravenous ranchers:

2 Tortilla – large flat, bread-type pancakes you can find in the supermarket bread section

½ A finely chopped Spanish onion

1 (400g) Tin chopped tomatoes

3 Cloves of minced garlic

4 Eggs

Vegetable oil for frying

A pinch of chilli powder

2 Chopped green chillis (or tablespoon of chopped Jalapeno chillis are best. You can buy them preserved if you can't get them fresh). More if you like hot things; but don't go berserk – it is breakfast, after all!

About 100g (4oz) grated cheese – 'Monterey Jack' would be authentic, but Cheshire or Cheddar cheese would do as well – don't use a mature cheese

Chopped Spring Onion greens – the green bits, not the white bits

When I first said to friends I am writing a book on breakfast a lot of my American friends said I should include this famous Mexican breakfast. The celebrity chef, Rick Stein, breakfast aficionado (get the pun?), has kindly helped me with this recipe. He has his version in his 'Food Heroes' book. The problem is, everybody has a different way to prepare Huevos Rancheros; and they all seem to be the authentic recipe and they all vary hugely. This is the way we like it in our neck of the woods:

METHOD

Put the tortilla breads onto a plate, cover with oiled foil or another inverted plate and put into a low, warm oven to heat through. In a frying pan or a wide-base saucepan, pour in a little oil, fry the onions for a few minutes, add the chilli powder and cook for a minute and then put in the tinned tomato and then, finally, the garlic. Cook for a minute then put in the chillis and simmer for at least 10 minutes so that the sauce reduces. (This could be done the night before if you want less fuss in the morning).

To serve; put a warm Tortilla on each plate, fry 4 eggs 'sunny side up' and place 2 on each Tortilla breads. Cover the eggs with hot sauce and sprinkle with cheese, scatter some chopped spring onion tops (not the white bottom bit) or chives over the cheese.

One of my New Mexico friends says he enjoys 'sausage' under his eggs – in America, sausage is not necessarily a sausage in a skin; it is usually fried, slightly spicy sausage-meat.

CARNE PICADA BURRITOS

INGREDIENTS

For 2 to 4 hungry cowboys - this produces 4 Burritos:

An onion, finely sliced. (I like to slice them from the pointy-end to the root-end, with the root cut out)

2 to 4 Jalapeño or green chillies, de-seeded and chopped (depending how hot you like it – 2 is just a hint of hot)

A little vegetable oil

450g (1lb) rump or rib eye steak cut into about 1cm (half inch) thick strips

½ teaspoon cumin

2 beef tomatoes, quartered, remove the seeds, and then chop the flesh into cubes

2 crushed cloves garlic

Salt and pepper

4 tortilla flat bread, warm them just before serving

4 eggs, scrambled

A Tex-Mex Brunch. This is a hot and spicy breakfast that is best served in the Summer, Al-Fresco. A friend of ours, from New Mexico, made this for our breakfast one summers morning in Sussex – we sat outside and gorged on these spicy wraps with mugs of black coffee. It is a wonderfully hot and spicy dish and jolts one into action, especially if you had rather a 'good' night before. This is another 'camp fire' type breakfast. You could make this well in advance and heat it up in a boat galley or on the prairie or in your garden in Sussex.

METHOD

Fry the onions and chillies for 5 minutes in a saucepan with a cover, stirring every now and then so that the onions do not colour too much. Remove from the saucepan and put to one side. Fry the steak strips for 2 minutes with the cumin and then add the onions and chillies, the tomatoes and the garlic. Season well and cook for 5 minutes over a medium heat.

To serve, lay one warm tortilla bread on each hot plate. Place a couple of tablespoons of Carne Picada down the centre of the bread, leaving a gap at one end. Spoon on some scrambled egg. Fold the piece of bread, where you have left a gap, over the mixture, then, fold over one side then the other, over the mixture so it is in a pocket of bread. Technically, you have created a sandwich, or 'wrap'. Serve hot immediately, its fantastic! Have a mug of steaming coffee (it has to be black – cowboys don't seem to use milk for some reason) and a huge napkin as you will get quite messy.

ITALIAN ALL DAY BREAKFAST CALZONE

INGREDIENTS

For 2 large calzones for 4 people

First the dough – you can buy pizza dough from the super market – but I like to make my own:

120ml (4 fl oz) warm (blood temperature) milk and water – half and half

2 teaspoons granulated sugar

2 teaspoons (1 X 7g sachet) easy-blend dried yeast

350g (12oz) Strong white bread flour

1 teaspoon salt

2 eggs

2 tablespoon extra virgin olive oil.

For the filling:

4 tablespoons tomato ketchup

6 cherry tomatoes cut in half

50g (2oz) sliced and the diced Prosciutto like Palma Ham or Speck

50g (2oz) sliced, cooked continental sausage such as Chorizo or Toulouse sausage

1 sliced Frankfurter sausage

1 large field mushroom, take off the stalk and fry in a little olive oil, then slice into thin slices

3 eggs scrambled; scramble the eggs only until just cooked, still creamy

1 tablespoons chopped fresh parsley, thyme and sage (or ½ teaspoon each of dried)

Salt and pepper

Extra virgin olive oil to drizzle over the top

There is nothing, in this world, in my view, nastier than an All Day Breakfast Sandwich from a service station on the motorway! I had to try one for my research and I could not even manage a mouthful. Call me 'picky' or just plain spoilt, but I think motorway service station sandwiches are awful, especially the All Day Breakfast Sandwich! So I make my own All Day Breakfast for long journeys early in the morning. Pippa is drumming her fingers and getting very shirty, dying to get on with the drive whilst I am cooking off our Calzones. A Calzone, I am sure most of you know, is a folded over pizza, like a Cornish pasty. More practical as a picnic brunch, and it is more Italian than British!

METHOD

Everything should be warm to encourage the dough to rise, so sift the flour and salt into a bowl and warm in an oven for a few minutes. Stir the sugar into the warm milk and water and when it has melted stir in the yeast. Leave the mixture to activate and form a foam on the top of the liquid. Whisk in the egg. Make a well in the warm flour and gradually stir in the liquid to form a dough. Add the olive oil and knead into the dough. Turn the dough out onto a floured surface and knead for at least 5 minutes. Leave the dough to prove for a couple of hours in a warm place, until it has doubled in size. You could also make the dough in a food mixer with a dough-hook or even a bread maker (you will have to follow the instructions of the machine). Pre-heat oven to 230°C, 450°F, gas mark 8 and put a non-stick baking tray into the oven to heat up.

Split the dough into two equal portions and roll them into a ball. Roll out each ball to a disk about 20cm (8 inch) discs. Split the filling into two and build the filling on one half of each disc. Sprinkle the herbs over last and drizzle a little olive oil over the filling. Brush the edges with water and fold the dough over the filling and crimp/pinch the edges together. Place the calzones onto the heated baking tray and bake for 8 to 10 minutes. Serve immediately or allow to cool and eat within a couple of hours.

I have also barbequed the calzones on a low-ish heat, it gave the calzone a very good flavour. It will take about 4 minutes on each side, turning after two minutes, turning the calzone a few degrees so that diamond shaped grill bar-lines are formed.

THE COLONEL'S RUMBLE TUMBLE EGGS (V,GF)

INGREDIENTS

For each person:

3 Free range eggs

A drop of milk

A big knob of butter (about a dessert spoon)

2 Spring onions, finely sliced

A heaped teaspoon of fresh grated ginger (optional)

A fresh red chilli, finely sliced with seeds if you like things spicy; or cut the chilli in half and remove the seeds (for less spicy) and then slice finely

Freshly ground pepper

One of our favourite guests enjoys this for his breakfast. He arrives at our B&B with his family for a weekend and is very particular about his breakfast – and quite rightly too! The Colonel tells me this is what the British eat in India. It can be either served as scrambled eggs or as a fluffy omelette (the fluffy bit is my idea).

METHOD

For scrambled: Whisk the eggs and the milk in a bowl. Melt the butter in a thick bottom saucepan, non-stick would be easier to clean. Put in the chilli, the onions, ginger and the ground pepper and fry gently on a low heat for a minute and a half. Pour in the egg and stir the mixture gently until you have creamy scrambled egg. Serve on crispy fried bread or toast.

For 'Rumble Tumble' Omelette: Use the same ingredients, except the egg whites are separated from the yolks and whisked to just firm (to 'soft-peak' condition; when the whites are not quite stiff enough to keep a point). Beat the yolk and milk together. Put a spoonful of whisked white into the yolks and mix thoroughly then very gently fold in the rest of the whisked whites with a plastic spatula, trying not to loose the air that has been whisked in.

Melt the butter in a thick bottom non-stick small frying or omelette pan. Put in the chilli, the onions, ginger and the ground pepper and fry gently on a low heat for a minute and a half. Pour in the eggs and stir with a wooden spoon a few times – very gently – and then leave on a gentle heat for a couple of minutes or until the bottom of the omelette is brown. Slide out onto a plate – don't fold as it should be fat and fluffy – sprinkle with chives and serve.

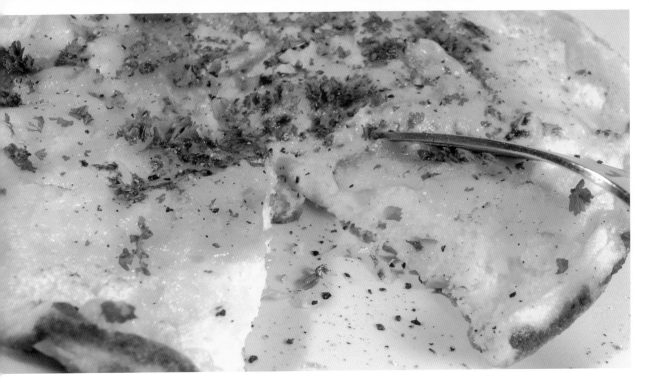

OMELETTE ARNOLD BENNETT (GF)

INGREDIENTS

For each person:

3 Free range eggs

A drop of milk

A big knob of butter (about a dessertspoon)

2 Spring onions, finely sliced

25g (1oz) Mature Cheddar cheese, grated

Freshly ground pepper

About 50g (2oz) lightly cooked smoked haddock – put the raw smoked haddock in a bowl, cover with milk and water, cling-wrap, put a small steam-slit in the wrap, microwave at full power for 3 minutes

2 Tablespoons double cream (optional)

Chopped parsley to decorate

Created for the writer Arnold Bennett. His penultimate novel, The Imperial Palace, was set in the Savoy Hotel in London. The hotel's head chef created the Omlette Arnold Bennett, which has remained on its menu ever since.

METHOD

Separate egg whites from the yolks of two of the eggs and whisk the whites to just firm (to 'soft-peak' condition when the whites are not quite stiff enough to keep a point). Beat the yolks and the remaining whole egg with the milk. Put a spoonful of whisked white into the yolks and mix thoroughly then very gently fold in the rest of the whisked whites with a metal spoon, trying not to loose the air that has been whisked in.

Melt the butter in a thick bottom non-stick small frying or omelette pan. Put in the onions, fry gently on a low heat for a minute and a half. Bring up the heat a little, pour in the eggs and stir with a wooden spoon a few times – very gently – and then leave on a gentle heat for a couple of minutes or until the bottom of the omelette is brown. Sprinkle over the flakes of cooked haddock, drizzle over the cream (leave it out if you are slimming!) and then the cheese and 'flash' under a grill to lightly melt the cheese and to lightly brown the top. Slide out the omelette onto a plate – you do not fold this omelette as it should be fat and fluffy – sprinkle with chopped parsley and serve with nothing.

EGG WHITE OMELETTE WITH WILD MUSHROOMS (V, GF)

INGREDIENTS

For each person:

You will need a small non-stick frying pan and a metal (even better; copper) whisking bowl, a glass one will do but not plastic!

Whisk up 4 whites with a teaspoon of water until the egg whites are quite fluffy but not so it is meringue consistency

Don't season – you should season after cooking with a little ground pepper

I had this at a very smart Hotel in New York. I had never heard of anything so decadent as an Egg White Omelette but it was light and very easy on the tummy – if you have a delicate stomach, or slimming, this is the Brunch for you. Egg whites have some protein, no cholesterol or fat and there are about 16.7 calories per egg white. I think I am right in saying that it is the only alkaline food product we eat!

METHOD

Heat up a couple of tablespoons of extra virgin olive oil in a frying pan and fry a handful of whole wild mushrooms. Turn the mushrooms out after lightly cooking and then wipe out the pan with kitchen paper. Season with a little salt and pepper.

Heat up another tablespoon more of olive oil, in the frying pan and then pour in the egg whites. With a folk, stir the egg white whilst gently shaking the pan until the egg has the consistency of runny scrambled egg white, then take out the fork. Try not to scrape the bottom of the pan with the fork too much (it doesn't do the non-stick much good). Allow the egg to cook until you can see the sides turning brown when you lift the edges.

Take the pan over to a hot plate, tip the pan up so that the omelette slides out and as it slides out, flip over the top edge and fold the omelette in half with the fork. Arrange the mushrooms to the side and sprinkle with chopped chives and parsley.

You could also serve this omelette with 'Salad with Fruit' (page 24), it would, therefore, be best to fry with groundnut oil or vegetable oil.

CODDLED EGGS IN A BREAD BASKET (V)

INGREDIENTS

For each person:

1 Small to medium,
free-range egg

A slice of sliced white
(square) bread

A tablespoon melted butter
or olive oil

A tablespoon double cream

Salt and ground pepper

A good Aga recipe. My mother made it for us in our ancient, wood-burning Aga in the school holidays – it always makes me happy when I have this breakfast. It can however be a bit fiddly. You dont have to coddle eggs in a bread basket, you can just pop them into a buttered ramekin and bake, but it is far less interesting!

METHOD

Pre heat oven 200°C, 400°F, gas mark 6 and bottom right of an Aga oven.

Break the egg into a ramekin (to check the yolk). Cut a slice of white bread – not too thinly, and remove the crusts. Roll the slice with a rolling pin to flatten the bread and then paint both sides with a little melted butter and cut in half from side to side leaving two fat rectangles. Press the rectangles into a lightly oiled, non-stick muffin baking tray, in a cross, forming a little basket then pour an egg into each basket with the tablespoon of double cream. Add plenty of seasoning. Put onto a baking tray and place in a hot oven. Check after 15 minutes, depending on the freshness of the egg, you might have to leave it for another 5 minutes. Some people enjoy a drop of Worcestershire Sauce and Tabasco on their eggs. They should have quite a soft yolk. If you prefer a harder egg, it is best to beat the egg and the cream before putting into the ramekins.

Rather go to bed supperless, than run in debt for a breakfast.

Benjamin Franklin

RAMEKINS OF HAM

INGREDIENTS

For 4 ramekins:

100g (4oz) lean cooked ham, finely chopped into little cubed

2 large eggs separated – yolks and whites

2 tablespoons sour cream

1 teaspoon made English mustard

A tablespoon chopped parsley

A pinch (quarter teaspoon) of ground mace

Salt and ground black pepper

Paprika – just a little to sprinkle over the top

Butter for greasing the ramekins well

This is a recipe I developed from an old recipe book I found called, 'Good Breakfasts' by Ambrose Heath (Faber & Faber 1940). The book is dedicated to the harsh times of war and how to make a breakfast with the 'shortages' or World War II – possibly something we might have to consider in this day and age!! Mr Heath includes such delicacies as Rabbit's Kidneys, Oyster Sausages (using oysters you find yourself on the beaches and rock pools) and Potted Head a kind of Brawn with a lambs head – not sure it's my kind of breakfast!

METHOD

Preheat oven to 180°C, 350°F, gas mark 4.

Place all – but the egg whites and the paprika – into a bowl and mix the ingredients together. Fill the ramekins three-quarters full. Place onto a baking tray and bake for 15 minutes, Meanwhile, whisk the egg whites to a 'soft peak' (so when you lift the whisks out the whites just come to a peak). Take the ramekins out of the oven, spoon on the whites equally over the ham mixture and sprinkle with a light dusting of paprika and place back in the oven for another 10 minutes. Serve immediately with toasted soldiers (strips of toast, for our American readers).

SPANISH EGG BREAKFAST FRITTATA

INGREDIENTS

For each person:

Two or three slices, finely chopped streaky bacon (smoked can be nice)

2 Thick slices (50g – 2oz) Chorizo sausage chopped into quarters (you can now get a good Chorizo at a good delicatessen or a deli counter at the supermarket)

A heaped tablespoon boiled potatoes cut into small cubes (roast potatoes from Sunday lunch will do if they were not over roasted)

2 Leaves of fresh sage (½ teaspoon dried)

2 Cherry tomatoes cut in half

2 Eggs whisked up with a dessertspoon of cream or milk

Salt and pepper

1 Finely sliced spring onion

I have been known to throw in a couple of tablespoons of cooked peas to add colour and taste

This is an easy breakfast for campers or a galley breakfast for sailors at sea.

METHOD

Fry the chopped bacon first until just cooked, if the bacon does not provide any fat (if you have only cheap supermarket bacon) add a little before putting in the Chorizo and little cubes of potato. Fry until turning brown, add the sage and then pour in the eggs. Keep stirring the mixture until the egg begins to cook then press in the halved cherry tomatoes, cut side up. Leave for a couple of minutes to brown. Put the Frittata under the grill if you like your eggs well done and serve it flat. Sprinkle with finely sliced spring onions.

The Spaniards use a kind of thick Parma ham instead of bacon which is fantastic but a little hard to find – unless you are in Spain! This is the kind of dish that is easy to eat with just a fork and tomato ketchup.

I wake up each morning and gather my wits
I pick up the paper and read the obits
If my name is not in it, I know I'm not dead
So I eat a good breakfast and go back to bed.

Studs Terkel

BACON JOLLY BOY

INGREDIENTS

For 2 people (4 pancakes):

2 Tablespoons plain flour

1/2 Teaspoon baking powder

1 Large egg

150ml (¼ pint) milk

Pinch of salt

4 Rashers of cooked streaky bacon, finely chopped

Vegetable oil to fry (my mother used lard, but it makes the pancakes a little heavy)

During the war, or when times were hard for country folk in the 'old days', this was a dish for when eggs were scarce. My mother used to do this for our breakfast and always said, as she produced these pancakes/omelettes, for her four boys; "These are Jolly Boys for my Jolly Boys, we used to have these during the war to make us jolly!" They are very good but I have always failed to see why they made you jolly.

METHOD

Whisk the batter ingredients (without the bacon) together to the consistency of thick cream. In a clean, thick-bottom, wide frying pan, pour in a couple of tablespoons of vegetable oil and bring it up to quite a hot heat, but not smoking. Pour in 50cl (about a quarter made) of the batter and tip the pan back and forth once so an oval, rather than a round shape is made in the pan. With a spatula, draw up two of the edges to form the oval shape. Leave to cook for a minute or until the underside is turning brown then sprinkle a quarter of the chopped bacon over the top. You don't toss this pancake, to cook the top you baste the oil over the top until just cooked and fluffed up. Slide onto a plate leaving as much oil as possible for the next 'Jolly Boy'.

'Jolly Boys' and baked beans was always a very evocative favourite of mine for breakfast or supper.

SMOKED SALMON AND ARTICHOKE FRITTATA (GF)

INGREDIENTS

For 4 people:

2 tablespoons olive oil

Half large red onions diced

100g (4oz) Artichoke hearts preserved in salt water, not vinegar

8 Eggs

150cl (4fl oz) Soured cream

100g (4oz) Chopped smoked salmon

1 tablespoon chopped fresh dill

Salt and pepper

It got me very excited how important a good quality breakfast is to the Americans, and they eat more better things for the body than I thought they did – Granola, fresh fruit yoghurts and Smoothies and vegetable omelettes or – the fashionable thing at the moment for breakfast in the US – are Frittatas. So from a recipe I found in a wonderful New England B&B Cookbook, whilst holidaying in Massachusetts, I have adapted this fashionable American breakfast:

METHOD

Preheat the 'broiler' (or grill). Heat the oil in a 10 inch (26cm) skillet or non-stick frying pan over a medium heat. Add the onions and cook without browning, then stir in the chopped and drained artichoke hearts. Beat together the eggs and cream and pour over the onions and artichokes. Stir with a fork until the eggs just begin to scramble, and then leave to cook, from the bottom up, on a medium heat for about 10 minutes. Sprinkle over the salmon, and most of the tablespoon of chopped dill, reserve a little for garnish, and season with salt and pepper (not too much salt), stir the salmon and dill a little into the egg. Lower the heat a little and cook for about another 5 to 10 minutes. Pull the egg away from the edges when it has cooked for about 4 minutes and check if it is browning. When it is three quarters cooked and the bottom is brown and firm and the top is still a little loose, place the pan under the grill to firm and brown a little. To serve, allow the Frittata to cool for a couple of minutes (the American for a 'couple' seems to be a little longer than '2' for some reason, so I would say 5 minutes), sprinkle over the reserved chopped dill, slice and serve.

I like to not make the Frittata too firm, so it is not dry. You could also dice up some boiled potatoes for extra texture or add some capers for a little 'bite'. This is a lovely supper dish as well and served with baked tomato, is wonderful. The Americans don't eat tomatoes for breakfast – only tomato ketchup. Viki tried to introduce them to a lovely half of baked tomato but none of the Americans would eat them! Strange how different we are in some things; The Americans and us Brits – but both cultures love breakfasts!

FLORENTINE EGGS

INGREDIENTS

For 4 Florentines:

4 tablespoons olive oil (or 2 to 4 heaped teaspoons butter – depending on you cholesterol levels)

500g (little over a pound) fresh spinach, cooked, with as much water as possible squeezed out – it cooks down to about 300g (11oz) cooked spinach

1 Finely sliced onion

2 Tablespoons double cream

1 Egg yolk

Salt and freshly ground black pepper

4 Large eggs

50g (2oz) of grated cheddar cheese or Hollandaise sauce (if you have the time hollandaise is very 'select' see page 38 for Hollandaise recipe)

A little dusting of grated nutmeg - optional

A nest of spinach bound together with eggs and cheese. We used to have a vegetarian part to our sandwich shop in London and 'veggies' queued up in the mornings, for hot Florentines - we sold them as fast as we made them!

METHOD

You will need 2 Le Creuset round oven dishes (the type pictured) or 4 round tart cases, (not the type with movable bottoms), or deep, oven-proof saucers. They should be between 10cm. to 15cm. (4" to 6") in diameter with a good lip around the edge.

Pre-heat the oven 190° C, 350 °F, gas mark 4.

Cook the spinach and squeeze out as much water as possible, put the spinach into a mixing bowel. Fry the onions so they do not take on any colour. Mix in with the spinach and allow to cool. Whisk in the egg yolk into the cream and mix in with the cooled spinach, with some salt and pepper. Place the oil or a knob of butter in each oven dish or tart case. Put the tart cases in the pre-heated oven for a couple of minutes to heat the oil or until the knobs of butter have melted. Divide the spinach equally between each of the hot tart cases, make a well in the centre to form a bird's nest, break an egg into each well and sprinkle the cheese over each egg. Put a pinch of nutmeg onto the grated cheese – (I hate nutmeg and I don't put any on mine, but, I am told it is very good and brings out the taste of the egg and spinach).

Place the tart cases or saucers onto a roasting tray and place in the oven on the top shelf for 20 to 25 minutes or 10 to 15 minutes if you like the yolk soft. Take the Florentines, out of the oven and serve with toasted sourdough bread.

BASIC EGGY BREAD (V)

INGREDIENTS

For each person;

1 Thick slice of bread

1 Large egg

1 Tablespoon of milk

1 Dessert spoon of castor sugar

Serve with sugar or maple syrup

METHOD

Eggy bread is a wonderful breakfast, one of my favourites – unfortunately, best for those who are thin! The Americans call it French Toast (I wonder if the French call it American Toast?!). Served mostly savoury, with bacon but just as nice served sweet:

For each person: A thick slice of bread – about an inch thick (2½ cm) cut in half. This works best with a 'Bloomer' loaf; brown or white. Whisk up a large egg and a tablespoon of milk (I sometimes use double cream), a dessert spoon of castor sugar for sweet. Soak the slices of bread in the egg for at least 4 minute to ensure the egg is soaked up in the bread. Put some oil or unsalted butter in a very hot frying pan and slide in the Eggy bread. Pour any egg left in the bowl over the top of the bread. Fry on one side for 30 seconds then turn it over and fry for another 30 seconds then reduce the heat by a quarter, turn the bread over and leave to cook slowly for two minutes on each side. Serve with sugar or Maple syrup, or Demerara sugar and lemon, or go savoury with some crispy pancetta.

Life, within doors, has few pleasanter prospects than a neatly arranged and well-provisioned breakfast table.

Nathaniel Hawthorne

FRENCH TOMATOEY TOAST (V)

INGREDIENTS

For 2 slices:

2 eggs

½ teaspoon salt

Freshly ground black pepper

A teaspoon Worcestershire sauce

50g (4oz) tomato ketchup

2 thick slices (1 inch or 2½ cm)
white or wholemeal bread

2 tablespoons vegetable oil

Chilli Flakes (optional)

METHOD

Like Eggy bread but with a little twist. Beat together the eggs, salt and pepper, the Worcestershire sauce and tomato ketchup with a couple of teaspoons of water. Soak the slices of bread in the mixture, if you like things spicy, sprinkle with a pinch of chilli flakes and then fry until brown in the vegetable oil. Serve hot with some lovely black pudding.

I went to a restaurant that serves "breakfast at any time".
So I ordered French Toast during the Renaissance.

Steven Wright

HAM AND EGG STRATA

INGREDIENTS

For 4 people:

4 thick slices white bread, crusts removed, cut into 2cm (½ inch) cubes

150g (6oz) thick-sliced and diced, smoked or un-smoked good boiled ham

1 tablespoon each: chopped fresh sage and chopped parsley (2 teaspoons of each dried)

5 large eggs

100ml (4fl oz) of full-fat milk (don't use semi-skimmed)

100ml (4fl oz) soured cream

1 teaspoon English mustard

Salt and pepper to season

This Brunch dish is called a 'Ham and Egg Strata' in America. When we put it on our Breakfast menu at our B&B in Cornwall, nobody had it. When we called it Ham & Egg Bread Pudding, it went like hot cakes! I thought people ate with their eyes, obviously the title of the dish counts for something as well. The Americans must have just got used to seeing 'Strata' on their menus. I mean 'Grits' – does that or does that not sound appetising to you? Grits is a very stodgy corn (maize) breakfast porridge, savoury or sweet and takes ages to make (not very nice, in my view)! But, would you order 'Grits' without knowing what it was?!

METHOD

Make the night before. You need a small buttered, deep casserole or oven-proof Pirex dish at least about 850ml to 900ml (1½ pints).

Toss the herbs in with the cubes of bread so they are evenly mixed. Place half of the bread cubes in the bottom of the buttered casserole. It is best to use dry, old bread – a very good way to use up old bread but not if it is starting to grow green bits! Sprinkle over the diced ham and cover with the rest of the bread cubes.

Whisk together the eggs, milk, cream and the mustard, seasoning. Pour it all over the bread and ham and cover with cling-wrap, place in the fridge over-night or for at least 3 hours.

Pre-heat the oven 190°C, 375°F, gas mark 5.

Place the casserole in the oven on a baking sheet and bake, uncovered for 40 minutes. Let it stand for 10 minutes before serving.

If you want to make it richer, sprinkle some grated cheese in with the ham with some chopped spring onions before putting on the top layer of herby bread cubes – not to my personal taste.

BAKING BRIOCHE (V)

INGREDIENTS

For 1 loaf:

12g (½ oz) fresh yeast –
I have tried and constantly failed
with dried, baking yeast and it
appears the real thing is best! If
all you have is dried yeast, follow
the instructions on the packet
implicitly

1 tablespoon caster sugar

50ml (2 fl oz) or 5 tablespoons
tepid milk

225g (8oz) strong white flour

½ teaspoon salt

100g (4oz) unsalted butter

2 large eggs

Brioche is a buttery bread the French enjoy, especially for breakfast. It is a difficult bread to make – nothing like as easy as ordinary bread! The dough is quite 'wet' and very difficult to handle – have a go. I once bought brioche from a supermarket and it was totally wrong – it was more like a cake; sweet, inedible and riddled with vanilla for some reason – tasted like solid, floury custard! If you live in the middle of the country, far away from the sophisticated metropolis, like we do, this is the only way you will obtain this wonderful, light breakfast bread.

METHOD

Cream the sugar and the yeast in a small mixing bowl. Use your warm fingers or a wooden spoon. Stir in the slightly warm, blood temperature milk and put to one side to allow the yeast to grow. Meanwhile, sieve the flour and salt into a food processor with the pastry blades installed. With the machine running, add the butter gradually in lumps and then the yeast mixture and the eggs. Mix to a soft dough, and continue to knead for at least a minute. Cover the bowl with oiled cling-film (so that the dough does not stick to it) and leave to 'prove' for at least an hour in a warm place. The dough should double in size.

Pre-heat the oven 190°C, 375°F, gas mark 5 (Aga bottom right).

When the dough has proved, 'knock back' or knead the dough again in the processor for another minute and then scrape out the dough into a buttered 450g. (1 lb.) loaf tin or a Brioche mould (a tin that looks like a giant fairy cake tin). Lightly dust the top of the dough with some flour and cover with a clean cloth, prove again for at least an hour. When it has proved, take off the cloth, gently place into the oven and bake for 35 to 40 minutes, cover the top with foil if it starts to turn too brown. Turn out on to a wire rack once baked and allow to cool.

Serve toasted Brioche with a Saucisse de Corbet (page 71) and some fried streaky bacon or Pancetta and an egg of your choice for a very continental Brunch or slice up some French sausages and make a sandwich with lots of Dijon Mustard (a Provencal Brunch). Or for the authentic French way; just dip toasted Brioche in a bowl of black coffee. You will then feel very Parisian and thin!

BRIOCHE FRENCH TOAST AND PEAR (V)

INGREDIENTS

Per substantial Frenchman:

A thick slice of Brioche, about 1½ cm (½ inch) thick

1 large egg

A teaspoon milk

A pear, peeled and cut in half

1 tablespoon unsalted butter

1 tablespoon soft brown sugar

Juice of a quarter of a lemon

1 tablespoon Cognac

A French Brunch that is more substantial than most French Breakfasts or Brunches. I now understand why all the French – well, the Parisians – are so thin. They don't eat anything substantial until supper, they only have a cigarette and black coffee when they get up in the morning!

METHOD

Beat the egg with the milk in a flat dish. Lightly toast the Brioche slice then soak both sides in the egg, ensure you soak up as much egg as possible. Melt half the butter in a clean frying pan over a medium heat. Add a teaspoon of oil to stop the butter burning. Fry the soaked slice – be careful, the Brioche is quite fragile and will probably need a spatula to ease it into the pan. Fry for a couple of minutes on each side. Cut the slice in half and fry the cut sides for another 30 seconds or until slightly coloured. Put the slice onto a hot plate, keep warm.

Remove the stalk and the core from the peeled pear and slice the pear into about 6 slices (depending how big the pear is), try not to cut all the way through at the stalk end – this will help to keep the 'fan' together. Fan out the slices. Melt the rest of the butter in the same frying pan, add the sugar. When the sugar has melted with the butter, bring up the heat and add the lemon juice, then the brandy and allow it to boil for a minute – you could set fire to it (Flambé – that is) – that will help get rid of the alcohol. Reduce the heat and gently put the pear-fan into the mixture and cook for about 30 seconds. After that, baste the sauce over the pear to cook the top a little. With a palette knife or good spatula, lift the pear out and place onto the plate with the Eggy Brioche. Spoon over some sauce over the pear, garnish with some grapes cut in half and serve.

My son suggested a dusting of icing sugar but I would find that too sweet – entirely up to you – and if you are young enough.

BRIOCHE AND MARMALADE PUDDING (V)

INGREDIENTS

For 4 to 6 people:

You will need a litre and a half to 2 litre casserole - butter generously all the sides

First soak 50g (2oz) golden sultanas in:

A cup of strong Earl Gray tea for at least 2 hours – the more the plumper they will get

10 square slices Brioche – (page 62) or light, white fluffy bread

50g (2oz) approx unsalted butter

Half a pound jar of thick-cut marmalade – possibly more if you love marmalade

Fine grated rind of half a lemon zest

Whisk together:

4 egg yolks and 1 whole egg

50g (2oz) caster sugar

200cl thick double cream

300cl Full fat milk

And to sprinkle on top:

Some melted unsalted butter

2 tablespoons of Demerara sugar mixed with half a teaspoon cinnamon (optional but brilliant for the winter

This is a lovely winter pudding for Brunch. I have done a version that is great all year round, but, if you replace the marmalade with Mincemeat, it makes a Christmas Brunch a little special. I have fiddled with this recipe for ages and I think, at last, I have cracked it. It has elements of an American Breakfast Casserole, a French pudding and a British Bread Pudding. Quite eclectic, really! Prepare the night before.

METHOD

Butter the slices of brioche with the unsalted butter – not too much as there is quite a lot of butter in the Brioche. Then spread lots of marmalade on 5 slices and sandwich them with the other slice – giving you five marmalade sandwiches. Cut each sandwich in half - into triangles. Lay a few triangles – pointy bit upwards – down the centre of the casserole, sprinkle some of the lemon zest over the sandwiches and then arrange the sandwiches around the edges sprinkling the rest of the lemon zest over. Push down the sandwiches so they fill the casserole. Pour over the egg and milk mixture and then cover with cling-wrap and put into the fridge to soak – for at least 3 hours or overnight.

Pre-heat oven 180°C, 350°F, gas mark 4.

In the morning, take out the casserole and remove the cling-wrap. Paint melted unsalted butter over any exposed bread crust and then sprinkle the sugar and the Demerara sugar. Put the casserole onto a baking sheet and bake for 50 minutes to an hour (keep an eye on the exposed sandwich peaks, don't let them burn). When you take it out, allow the casserole to sit for 10 to 15 minutes and then serve. It is lovely with an orange salad (page 25) or a compote (page 23) or just on its own with a dash of cream.

HAWAIIAN BREAKFAST (V)

INGREDIENTS

For 2 people:

2 croissants cut in half or 2 thick slices of white bread

2 large eggs

A dash of milk

1 slice of fresh pineapple, the core removed and chopped

About a dozen green grapes (preferably seedless) sliced in half

2 tablespoons sliced toasted almonds

3 tablespoons crème fraiche

1 tablespoon runny honey

2 tablespoons desiccated coconut

A knob of unsalted butter and a dash of oil

A few fresh blueberries or redcurrants

Think of a wonderful tropical beach, a dusky maiden (or hunk) with a huge smile and this exotic breakfast, she/he serves you at a table at the waters edge with little waves lapping at your toes – what a wonderful morning. A Brunch just as enjoyable in a flat in Clapham in February! This is not particularly fattening if you use low fat crème fraiche and is also a very good way of getting fruit into fussy children in the morning!

METHOD

In a flat bottomed pudding bowl break in the eggs and beat lightly with a dash of milk. Soak the cut side of the croissants in the beaten egg (or each side of the bread with the mixture, try to give each slice an equal soaking). Put the pineapple, grapes and coconut into a mixing bowl, mix in the almonds, honey and finally crème fraiche. The crème fraiche will loosen up with the juice from the fruit.

Melt the butter with a touch of oil to stop it burning, in a clean frying pan, over a medium heat. Slide the croissants soaked in egg into the frying pan, eggy side of the croissants down, fry until golden brown. Put the croissants onto plates – eggy side up. Place the pineapple mixture in the centre of the croissants (or eggy bread). Serve immediately with a sprinkle of blueberries or redcurrants to decorate.

BLINIS FOR BRUNCH (V)

INGREDIENTS

To make 12 to 15 Blinis:

150ml (¼ pint) warm milk

½ teaspoon dried yeast or
6g (¼oz) fresh yeast

1 teaspoon sugar

175g (6oz) plain four or, if you
can find it, buckwheat flour

1 large egg

Pinch of salt

Oil for frying

Blinis are a little pancake from Russia made with buckwheat – a gluten free grain, related to rhubarb, not, as one supposes, to wheat. It is more of a bread than a pancake. In Russia, you would cover your Blinis with soured cream and Caviar (see page 67). You can serve blinis with tons of things for Brunch; smoked salmon and scrambled egg; cottage cheese and jam and many other things; there are a couple of other suggestions below.

METHOD

Put the yeast into a bowl (crumble fresh yeast) and add the sugar, pour in the warm (body temperature) milk. Whisk the milk and the yeast to mix thoroughly and leave in a warm place for at least 10 minutes – until there are bubbles over the surface of the milk.

Sift in the flour into a mixing bowl with a pinch of salt. Whisk the egg into the milk and yeast. With a hand-whisk, beat in the milk mixture into the flour gradually, until a thick batter forms. Allow the batter to rest for 10 minutes. Heat a small amount of vegetable oil in a thick bottom pan or skillet, and spoon in one dessertspoon of the batter. If you find the batter is too thick after resting (sticks to the spoon - does not pour off the spoon), slacken it off by whisking in a little more milk – but not too much. Flatten out the batter a little and allow the batter to firm up and then flip over the Blinis and fry the other side. It will puff up into a bready-type, small pancake and ready to serve.

It is best not to store blinis but to eat them the day you make them. Shop-bought blinis have some sort of preservative in them that ensures they keep their rather unappetising rubberyness!

BLINIS WITH CAVIAR, SERVED 'POLONAISE'

INGREDIENTS

2 hard-boiled eggs

A tablespoon finely chopped parsley and capers

4 Blinis - the flatter, the better (Page 66). You could use Scotch Pancakes or Drop Scones for these snacks except they may be a little too sweet

4 teaspoons soured cream

½ teaspoon cream of horseradish

4 teaspoons Caviar (or lumpfish caviar, for economy)

METHOD

Place 2 eggs in a saucepan of warm water, bring to the boil and boil for 8 minutes. Immediately, plunge the eggs in cold running water and leave the eggs in the cold water until they are cold. Prepare the eggs 'Polonaise' – an old fashioned accompaniment for Caviar: cut the eggs in half and remove the yolks. The yolks should not have any grey on them, if they have; they have been cooked too long or they are not very fresh. Finely chop up the yolks and the white, keep them separate. Arrange on a nice platter; the chopped egg yolk, then the chopped whites, the chopped parsley and capers and finally, a couple of teaspoons of Caviar. You could present then in four quarters of a circle.

Mix the horseradish with the soured cream and place in a little bowl. Put some crushed ice in a large bowl and put the plate with the Caviar Polonaise on top to keep cool.

To serve the Caviar; there should be two silver teaspoons (or Mother of Pearl for pure elegance, as pictured). Keep everything cold; spoons, bowls and plates. Serve the Blinis whilst they are still warm. What luxury, what decadence you should always serve Champagne or, for true authenticity, vodka served in a block of ice: If you have an old gallon ice cream tub; fill it with water (use filtered water as it will give you clear ice), put the bottle into the centre of the tub (you might have to secure it with some string or sticky tape), pop it in the freezer so that the water freezes round the bottle – this will take a couple of days. Pop the block out of the ice cream tub just before serving.

HAM AND MARMALADE BLINIS

INGREDIENTS

4 quite large Blinis (page 66)

Unsalted butter, slightly softened or olive oil-type low-fat spread

4 teaspoons thick-cut traditional marmalade. Chop up the 'shreds' a bit, so it is not too lumpy

50g (2oz) good, sliced, smoked ham

2 tablespoons crème fraiche or cream cheese

Tablespoon chopped fresh sage

Ground pepper

METHOD

Spread butter or low-fat spread on one side of 4 blinis. Take a pastry cutter that is the same size as the blinis and cut 4 discs of ham. Finely chop up the bits of ham that are left over and mix in the crème fraiche or cream cheese. Place a disc of ham on each of the four buttered blinis, spread half a teaspoon of marmalade on each ham disc, divide the cream cheese and ham mixture and place a dollop in the centre of the marmalade. Scatter a little chopped sage on each lump of cream cheese and finally a very light sprinkle of freshly ground pepper.

Once a woman has forgiven her man, she must not reheat his sins for breakfast.

Marlene Dietrich

BRUNCH ON A STICK

INGREDIENTS

For 4 kebabs, 2 hungry people:

You will need 4 skewers, either bamboo ones that you first soak in water for an hour and then brush them with oil, or, 4 metal sewers that you brush with oil

2 thick slices of good white bread – about 2 cm (½ inch) thick, wholemeal if you are feeling healthy, cut into 2cm cubes with the crust left on. I like to use open textured French bread. Try not to use close textured, plastic supermarket bread

4 tablespoons good extra virgin olive oil with a pinch of salt and freshly ground pepper

100g (approx.) cheese - Haloumi Cypriot Cheese is best or Swiss cheese; cut into 2cm cubes

2 Thick slices of cooked ham, cut into 2 cm squares

100g (approx) Chorizo sausage – try and get the thin 2cm sausage

8 cherry tomatoes

8 to 16 large fresh sage leaves

2 tablespoons olive oil, a teaspoon lemon juice and a tablespoon butter melted with some salt and pepper to brush over the kebabs.

Mock Hollandaise Sauce:

300ml (½ pint) Low Fat Mayonnaise

½ teaspoon prepared English mustard

2 egg whites

Salt and freshly ground pepper

2 Tablespoons lemon juice

A very simple Brunch that you can prepare the day before. All you need to do is light the bar-b-que in the morning and put on the kebabs. Keep an eye on these kebabs; I managed to set fire to some I was cooking when I was not looking and filled the whole neighbourhood with smoke, one still Sunday morning. These kebabs can also be cooked under the grill – possibly safer for the neighbourhood!

METHOD

Put the bread cubes into a bowl and pour over the olive oil and seasoning. Mix thoroughly so that the oil covers the bread cubes. Thread the cubes of bread (put the skewer through the crust for some stability,) cheese, sage leaf, ham, sausage, another sage leaf, whole cherry tomato and another cube of bread on each skewer then, if you have room, repeat the combination. You can do this the day or evening before to save time or a sleep-in. Light the bar-b-que and wait until the flames have died away and just the embers are glowing.

Melt the oil, lemon juice and butter mixture and brush some over the kebabs. Put the kebabs onto the bar-b-que and keep an eye on them. They will need turning quite a lot and keep an eye on the cheese. Keep basting with the oil and butter mixture. The kebabs will be ready when the bread has turned brown and the cheese has slightly melted. Slide off the skewer onto the plate. The tomatoes are likely to burst if you put too much pressure on them. Serve with Scrambled Egg or:

Serve with Mock Hollandaise Sauce (Low Cholesterol):

In a small saucepan of hot water, place a glass bowl over the water (not touching the water) into which you whisk all ingredients until smooth. Stirring constantly, cook over medium-low heat until thick.

TEXAN STEAK N' EGGS – WITH POTATO HASH

INGREDIENTS

For the Potato Hash for 2 people:

150g (6oz) peeled and grated potato

½ teaspoon salt

A couple of grinds of the pepper mill

1 egg

1 level tablespoon crème fraiche or clotted cream

2 tablespoon chopped spring onions – green bits as well or fresh chives

A tablespoon beef dripping or vegetable oil

You will need 2 to 4 Chef's Rings about 2 ¾ inch wide by 1 ½ inch deep (7cm X 3.5cm)

Steak and eggs are a typical Cowboy-style breakfast. I love steak for breakfast, in particular, Rump steak; it has a lot of taste and is the better steak to fry. Imagine waking up in the Texan wilderness, slapping half a cow into a 'skillet' over an open fire, and serving it up, topped with a few fried eggs and lashings of tomato ketchup whilst listening to the Coyotes baying in the distance and the screech of a Bald Headed Eagle overhead. Unfortunately, you are not likely to be able to have delicious Potato Hash Cakes if you are out in the desert!

METHOD

Preheat the oven 230°C, 450°F, gas mark 8.

Grate the potato onto a clean tea towel and sprinkle with the salt and mix the salt in with the potato and leave for it to think about life for a couple of minutes. The salt will draw out the moisture. Put the beef dripping into a small frying pan over a medium heat. Whilst the pan is heating up, fold the edges of the tea towel over the potato; twist the ends of the tea towel clockwise one end, anticlockwise the other end to form a towel-cracker. Keep twisting until all the potato juice is squeezed out of the grated potato. Squish it with yours hands if you are strong enough. If you have squashed as much of the juices from the potato, turn the potato out into a dry bowl, add ground pepper, egg, crème fraiche, spring onions or chives and mix it all up. Increase the heat under the frying pan, place two chef's rings in the pan (or two empty food tins with the top and bottom removed) and fill each ring equally with the potato mixture. Press the mixture into the rings. Fry for 2 minutes or until it browns. Push out the cake, out of the ring (if they stick a bit, run a knife round the inside of the ring), and turn the cake over and brown the other side. Now put the cakes onto an oiled or non-stick baking sheet and bake in the oven for 5 minutes until golden brown. Keep warm for the steak. If you allow the cakes to cool after the frying stage, you then heat them up again in the oven for 10 minutes, they will be crunchy on the outside and fluffy in the inside.

I like to fry steak rather than grill; it seals in the juices quicker. A trick to frying steak to your liking is by prodding the steak with your forefinger, then the fleshy bit of the thumb muscle on your hand – that is 'Blue to Raw'. Now, put you thumb onto your forefinger and prod the steak, then the 'fleshy bit' – and that is rare. As your thumb touches each finger, up to your little finger, the 'fleshy bit' gets harder and harder and is about the same as the degrees of well-doneness of the steak: Fore-finger – rare; middle finger – medium; ring finger – medium well; little finger well-done or ruined (in my view).

Serve with a couple of fried eggs and the Potato Hash Cake.

SAUCISSE DE CORBET

INGREDIENTS

For 12 Saucissons:

225g (8oz) dry-cured belly pork like Italian Pancetta or French 'Lardons'

225g (8oz) lean pork meat like a leg or loin of pork

110g (4 oz) beef suet. This is to make the sausage juicy; if there is lots of fat on the belly pork, reduce the amount of suet by half

75g (3oz) white breadcrumbs

½ a teaspoon each: salt, garlic salt and ground white pepper

1 tablespoon granulated sugar

100ml (4fl oz) full red wine, preferably French

A tablespoon of fresh chopped parsley or 2 teaspoons of dried

I like to put a pinch of Ground Bay in the mixture but it is virtually impossible to find! If you can get it, put in a pinch (and perhaps you can send a little to me!)

A skinless sausage easily home made, but with more of a French influence. In fact the recipe came from a 'Boucherie' in a southern French town, near where my father now lives in his dotage. The butcher asked if I could call the sausage after the town he lived in – he was very disappointed when I told him it was impossible; mainly because he lived in the charming Gascony town of 'Condom'! So I have called it after my father's house. I have had to adapt this quite a lot as it is impossible to find Saltpetre in the UK and the French cure bacon slightly differently.

METHOD

Mince or finely chop the meat. The typical Toulouse sausage has course minced meat, so, if you have a big mincing dye for your mixer, all the better, otherwise, chop it up by hand as small as you can, but not too small.

Put all the ingredients in a mixing bowl and mix together thoroughly. The best way is to 'squidge' the mix through your (washed) hands. Ensure you get it all mixed together, then divide the mix into 12 (about 60g just over 2 ounces) lumps. Knead each lump of the mix a little and then shape into a sausage about 10cm long by about 2 cm thick (4 inches x ¾ inch).

Fry or grill the sausages only after they have rested in the fridge overnight or at least 2 hours. Cook them slowly over a moderate heat for about 10 to 15 minutes. Serve them the Provençal way, hot, in a roll with a little olive oil and sliced tomatoes – or just with an egg.

BRUNCH CLUB SARNI

INGREDIENTS

To produce 4 good-size sandwiches:

A medium -sliced loaf square white bread (it has to be white!).

50g (2oz) Soft butter

2 large beef tomatoes, skinned; by putting into boiling water for a minute until the skin blisters and easy to peal off, then sliced thinly

A small whole free-range chicken, poached (see below)

8 to 12 rashers streaky bacon, grilled until crispy

4 to 6 tablespoons mayonnaise

A Coz or Romaine lettuce, washed

6 slices of good, un-smoked ham

6 finely sliced large gherkins

Salt and pepper

Poached Chicken:

For a chicken of up to 2 kilos (5lbs.):

2 tablespoons vegetable oil

1 large carrot roughly chopped

1 large onion cut into quarters - skin still on

1 celery stalk, roughly chopped

2 cloves garlic crushed

6 black peppercorns

1 bay leaf

A couple of sprigs of various herbs, tied together to make a Bouquet Garni

1 heaped teaspoon sea salt

A very strange thing to include in a Brunch Book, you might think. But I had some pressure to include a club sandwich from friends Hugh and Sarah, who insist it is, certainly, an essential part of their Brunch on a Sunday Morning. Even if you don't regard this as a Brunch – it is, possibly, the best way to do a Club sandwich for a picnic, a desk lunch or even a 'Latefast' (something for the early hours of the morning). The Mayonnaise must be home made, the bacon is best crispy and the chicken poached. I used to have a sandwich shop in the City of London and we always poached the chicken as it kept the flesh very juicy.

METHOD

In a big saucepan, with a lid, put in the oil and the vegetables fry for 5 to 10 minutes, over a high heat stirring a few times. Allow the onions to brown a little. Add the Bouquet Garni, peppercorns and the whole chicken. Cover with hot water, ensuring the cavity in the chicken fills with water, put on the lid, bring to the boil and simmer for 15 minutes. Remove the heat and leave the chicken in the water with the lid on for at least 45 minutes. When it is cool put the whole lot in the fridge until you need the chicken.

You can leave the chicken in the stock overnight. Take the chicken out of the stock, strip off any skin and throw it away. Take the meat off the bones and put the bones back into the stock. You can use the stock again for poaching within a day or two as long as you keep the stock cold in the fridge or you could boil it up and freeze it.

If you only need chicken for one or two sandwiches, remove the skin off a chicken breast or a breast and a thigh. Chop up a carrot, half a onion, crush a clove of garlic, and with a Bouquet Garni, put into a small saucepan, with the chicken, cover with cold water, bring to the boil then reduce to a simmer for 10 minutes then allow to cool for an hour in the water/stock.

To construct each Club Sarni: Toast 3 slices of white bread. Butter 2 slices. On the first buttered slice; lay 3 or 4 slices of tomato, then take some chicken meat and pull apart into thin shreds – I prefer the chicken to be shredded rather than sliced. Now put on two or three rashers of crispy bacon, spread some mayonnaise of a second slice of bread and press it – mayo-side down – onto the bacon. Spread some more mayonnaise over the other side of the second slice and cover with a leaf or two of Coz lettuce. Cover the lettuce with a slice of ham, then sprinkle some sliced gherkins over the ham. Season with salt and pepper and put the other buttered slice on top. Put a long cocktail stick through each sandwich quarter, so that it does not all fall apart when you cut into quarters (4 triangles). Put an olive on each protruding stick so 'Health and Safety' don't give you a hard time with pointy sticks getting stuck in people's mouths!

OYSTER PO' BOYS

INGREDIENTS

For 2 to 4 sandwiches depending on greed:

1 French Bread long loaf (not the thinner French Baguette)

50g (2oz) melted butter

4 tablespoons mayonnaise

4 Coz or iceberg lettuce leaves, shredded

12 to 15 Pacific large oysters (or native, smaller and tastier Falmouth or Kentish oysters – they are quite expensive and you would need about 24 - get your fishmonger to open them. Or you could also use about 30 little Queen scallops)

2 tablespoons plain flour seasoned with: 1 teaspoon of each: salt, white pepper and ½ teaspoon paprika

For the tempura batter:

200ml (7fl oz) soda-water (sparkling water is ok but is not quite fizzy enough)

1 egg

100g (4oz) plain flour

50g (2oz) cornflour

½ teaspoon salt

Vegetable oil for deep-frying

1 tablespoon capers (optional garnish)

A dusting of cayenne pepper

One of the popular Cajun sandwiches from New Orleans. Possibly, from the French phrase 'pourboire' meaning a 'tip' or a drink, not for a waiter but for the stroppy wife who has been waiting up all night for her gambling husband! For a few cents you could buy a Po'Boy as you lurch your way home – oysters are cheap in the southern States of America. This is a very good 'Latefast' or Brunch sandwich – it is said to have aphrodisiac properties!

METHOD

Firstly; put the batter flour, cornflour and salt into a sieve and sift into a largish mixing bowl. Put all the batter ingredients into a fridge to get very cold: This is a trick that my friend Rick Stein tells us to do to ensure a crisp batter.

Pre-heat the oven to 230°C, 450°F, gas mark 8.

Slice the French Bread nearly all the way through, lengthways and pull out the flesh - leaving a little bit of the white flesh, about 1 cm (¼ inch). Brush the insides of the loaf with the melted butter and place in the oven on a baking tray for 5 minutes or until crisp and golden inside the loaf, allow to cool a bit. Spread the mayonnaise over the inside of the baguette and lay the shredded lettuce into the bottom half of the baguette.

Pre-heat the oil so it is quite hot (not smoking hot).

Make the batter just before you are going to serve. Take all the ingredients out of the fridge, make a well in the flour and break in the cold egg and then whisk in the soda-water, whisk a few times – it does not matter if there are a few lumps and it does not need to rest. Get the oysters out of their shell, dust them with the seasoned flour, then dip each oyster in the batter (it will coat the oyster only thinly) and drop the battered oysters into the hot oil. Fry for 3 minutes then put onto kitchen paper. You might have to do this in three batches so, keep the cooked oysters warm.

Arrange the brown oysters onto the shredded lettuce, sprinkle the capers over the top and lightly dust with the cayenne, press the halves together, cut into 2 or 4 and serve hot immediately, wrapped in a napkin.

I can remember eating something similar in Marseilles, when I was youth travelling around France. It was being sold out of a van in the early hours of the morning on the dockside and, ever since I have enjoyed this for breakfast. They put capers in with their Po'Boy – but they called it something else - I can't remember what it was called but it was magic.

THE SPORTSMANS (AND WOMAN'S) BREAKFAST

INGREDIENTS

For 2 to 4 people, depending on appetite:

1 Small white Bloomer loaf – about a foot (30cm) long

A good dollop (50g/2oz) of butter for spreading

1 Tablespoon English mustard

2 Tablespoons vegetable oil

1 Large Spanish onion peeled and finely sliced

1 Tablespoon green peppercorns, drained of the brine they come in and slightly crushed

1 Tablespoon mushroom ketchup or Worcestershire sauce

350g to 400g (12oz to 14oz) rump steak

2 Tablespoons tomato chutney or relish

Salt and pepper

A meaty sandwich – very good for Picnic Breakfast! I go fishing and shooting just so I can have this sandwich for breakfast. I am terrible at both sports but very good at eating the sandwich. Best made the day or evening before – served cold or slightly warm from keeping it in your back pocket!

METHOD

Cut the small bloomer in half lengthways but not all the way through. Open the bread up and liberally spread with butter. Spread the mustard over the bottom half of the Bloomer. Heat up the oil in a frying pan and fry the onions on a high heat for a minute, stirring all the time. Turn down the heat and fry for a further 15 minutes, over a low heat stirring every other minute or so; allow the onions to brown slightly. Whilst the onions are cooking, season the steak and beat it with a tenderising hammer, add green peppercorns for the last couple of minutes of frying the onions. Spoon out the onions, and green peppercorns onto the mustard side of the Bloomer, leaving as much of the oil in the pan as possible. Spread out the onions and close the bread whilst you fry the steak. Fry the steak for about 30 seconds on a high heat on each side to seal in the juices, then reduce the heat and cook for about 4 minutes each side for a medium rare steak (longer if you want it less rare – but the more you cook it the less juicy it is. As soon as the steak is cooked, put it onto a plate (so that you can keep the juices) and carve the steak into slices. Make sure you do this quickly to keep the steak hot. Arrange the steak in the bloomer on the onions, pour all the carving juices over the top, season and sprinkle the mushroom ketchup over the top of the steak, spoon on the tomato chutney.

Now, wrap the sandwich up very tightly with cling-film and place in the fridge overnight. This has all got to happen pretty rapidly as the juices and the butter has to melt and mingle.

To serve – unwrap the sandwich the next morning and wrap it up tightly again in greaseproof paper. Tie some string or raffia around it to keep the pressure on. When you are ready to eat it cut into 2 or 4 and serve with game chips (thick crisps) and a flask of coffee (or sloe gin!). This will get you going for any sporting event. The juices form a slight jelly and the flavours have mingled with the bread.

DEVILLED KIDNEYS AND POACHED EGG

INGREDIENTS

For 4 people:

8 prepared lambs kidneys, cut in half a cored

25g (1oz) butter and a drop of oil

A little cayenne pepper

For the sauce:

100ml (4fl oz) Red wine vinegar

2 tablespoons granulated sugar

1 tablespoon Worcestershire sauce

1 teaspoon English mustard

½ teaspoon paprika

½ teaspoon salt

Freshly ground pepper

25g (1oz) more butter

(2 tablespoons double cream – optional)

To serve:

4 thick slices white fried bread; fry and then leave in a warm oven on kitchen paper - the slices will become quite crispy.

1 tablespoon fresh chopped parsley.

4 large eggs poached. Or 4 small duck eggs, also poached.

Cayenne pepper

Just a wonderful Brunch for us Trenchermen and carnivores. One can imagine arriving down to Brunch at a stately home and running through the chafing dishes with indifferent interest, until, you raise the lid of the Devilled Kidneys, which emits a delicious piquant and savoury aroma. Devilled Kidneys is the epitome of Brunch. It also makes a great supper snack in front of the telly!

METHOD

Fry the cleaned kidneys (the butcher will prepare them for you) on both sides in the oil and butter for about 3 to 4 minutes on each side, over a medium heat. Take the cooked kidneys out of the pan with a slotted spoon, leaving the juices behind. Keep the kidneys warm.

Bring up the heat and stir in the red wine vinegar and the sugar. Cook for a couple of minutes and then add the rest of the sauce ingredients, leaving the butter to last. Bring to the boil and allow the sauce to boil for only a minute, stirring all the time. Taste for seasoning. Return the kidneys to the sauce and simmer on a very low heat for a minute (more if you like the kidneys well cooked and not slightly pink). It has been known to add double cream to the sauce at this stage but I find it makes it far too rich – I leave it to you.

Poach the eggs (see page 36). Place a slice of crispy fried bread on each plate. Just before serving the kidneys, stir in the chopped parsley. Equally spoon out the devilled kidneys onto the centre of the fried bread, with a little sauce. Lay a poached egg on the top, dust some cayenne pepper over the yolk and serve immediately.

DEVILLED FIELD MUSHROOM & POACHED EGG (V)

INGREDIENTS

For 2 to 4 people:

4 large field or morel mushrooms. It would be an advantage if they each were slightly cupped. Remove the big stalk in the middle. If you are fortunate to have a Puff Ball mushroom, this makes an exceptional Devilled Dish

25g (1oz) Butter

2 Tablespoons extra virgin olive oil

4 Large eggs

A little cayenne pepper

For the sauce:

2 More tablespoons extra virgin olive oil

150ml (¼ pint) Red wine vinegar

Juice of ½ a lemon

2 Tablespoons caster sugar

1 Tablespoon mushroom ketchup or Worcestershire sauce

½ Teaspoon English mustard

½ Teaspoon smoked paprika

½ Teaspoon salt

Freshly ground pepper

4 Pikletts – a cross between a crumpet and an English muffin – they are sometimes available in the larger supermarkets, or 4 slices of thin white bread, crusts removed, fried to a deep gold and crispy

Watercress and Cayenne pepper for decoration

A vegetarian version of a very old fashioned breakfast – devilled kidneys. If you prefer the carnivorous version – it's the same as this but with kidneys!

METHOD

Fry the mushrooms in the olive oil and butter, gill side down to start with, for two minutes, and then gently turn them over, fry for another 2 to 3 minutes over a medium heat. Remove the mushrooms when they are cooked and beginning to flatten out, keep warm. Put all the sauce ingredients in a bowl, mix and then pour into the pan the mushrooms were fried in. Bring to a simmer and reduce the sauce for about five to seven minutes. The sauce should be well reduced but not syrupy. Check the seasoning. When you have made the devilled sauce, pour over the gills of the mushroom cups and allow the sauce to soak in for a couple of minutes.

Poach the eggs (see page 36).

Place a poached egg on each mushroom. Put each mushroom onto a toasted Picklett or on a slice of crispy fried bread. Decorate with watercress and a dusting of Cayenne pepper on the egg yolks. Drizzle any sauce that is left over around the mushrooms in that 'Cheffy' way. Eat immediately before the bread gets too soggy.

There is a vast difference between the savage and the civilised man, but it is never apparent to their wives until after breakfast.

Helen Rowland

POTTED SALMON AND FAIRY TOAST

INGREDIENTS

Serves 6 to 8

100g (4oz) butter

A teaspoon blades mace or a good pinch (½ teaspoon) of ground mace

A good pinch (½ teaspoon) cayenne pepper

4 scrapes freshly grated nutmeg

A teaspoon anchovy essence

A teaspoon Worcestershire sauce

Freshly ground black pepper

500g (1lb 2oz) fresh wild (if possible) salmon, skinned and diced into small 1cm (¼ inch) cubes

50g (2oz) unsalted butter for clarified butter

8 thick slices of white or wholemeal bread

Popular dish with both shrimps (better known as a starter for dinner) and salmon. It makes a very good Brunch dish. If you make it into a one large terrine that all have to share, it gets the morning conversation going. If, however, you are a believer of no morning conversation, just a newspaper as companion, pot the salmon into ramekins. Best to be made the previous day or so.

METHOD

Melt the butter in a large saucepan and add the spices, allow the spices to infuse for a minute or so over a gentle heat, then add the anchovy essence, Worcestershire sauce, a couple of grinds of black pepper, bring nearly to the boil and then stir in the salmon cubes, gently. Take off the heat and allow the salmon heat through for a couple of minutes, stirring only once or twice very gently. You don't want the salmon to break up too much and loose the cubes.

Spoon out the mixture into 6 ramekins or a Kilner sealed jar, press gently down and put into a fridge to solidify. Melt the unsalted butter slowly until you can see the solids separate. Pour off the clarified butter onto the top of the potted salmon. Place the ramekins in the fridge for a couple more hours or overnight.

To serve; toast the sliced bread. Cut off the crusts and slice the slices into two thin slices. Grill the un-toasted side until crisp – you will have to keep an eye on them as they turn to burnt very quickly. Serve the Fairy Toast (you could pretentiously call it Melba Toast) on the side.

I once did this with cubes of salmon and monkfish to great effect. You will need to cook the monkfish first for a little longer than the salmon. You could also use a pint of peeled brown shrimp for a dinner party starter as well as Brunch.

KOULIBIAC

INGREDIENTS

For 6 to 8 hungry Cossacks:

500g (1lb 2oz) approx. de-frosted ready made puff pastry

50g (2oz) Couscous (dry weight). Traditionally, Bulgur wheat or rice is used – couscous is slightly lighter

2 Large lightly, hard boiled eggs (brought to the boil from cold and then boiled for 6 to 8 minutes – depending how fresh the eggs are – so the yolk is still a little soft-ish)

50g (2oz) Unsalted butter

1 Tablespoon vegetable oil

1 Large Spanish onion, finely sliced

3 or 4 Large morel or field mushrooms, sliced

1 Heaped tablespoon fresh dill, chopped

1 Heaped tablespoon fresh flat leaf parsley roughly chopped

350g (12oz) Fresh salmon, in ¼ inch cubes. Sturgeon is traditionally used but a little unobtainable in the UK!

Grated rind of ½ a lemon

3 Tablespoons soured cream

Cayenne pepper, salt and black pepper

A beaten egg for glazing

A traditional Russian breakfast that I have adapted from a recipe I found in a Czechoslovakian cookbook. For some reason the author is not credited.

METHOD

The previous evening would be the best time to prepare this breakfast as it is quite involved. Melt the butter and the oil in a pan and fry the onions for about five minutes, don't brown. Add the mushrooms and fry for a couple of minutes, stirring all the time allowing the juices to soak into the mushrooms, put the lot into a bowl, allow the mix to cool. Put the couscous into a bowl and cover with boiling water, leave to soak, fluff the grains up a bit and leave to cool. Roll out the pastry on a floured surface into a long rectangle of about 23cm (9in) by 56cm (22in) and cut in half, 2 rectangles 23cm X 28cm. Place one rectangle onto an oiled baking sheet or on baking parchment. Spoon half the couscous onto the middle of the rolled dough and form a rectangle of couscous leaving a border of dough of about a good 2½ cm (1 inch) around the edge. Spoon on half the mushroom mix neatly on top of the couscous then the eggs (that you have peeled and sliced thickly), now scatter the chopped herbs, seasoning and cayenne pepper. Keeping the flat, rectangle shape as neat as possible - pile the fish cubes on top of the stack, sprinkle the lemon rind, some more seasoning and then pour over the soured cream. Spoon on the rest of the mushrooms and the couscous and season again.

Preheat the oven 220°C, 425°F, gas mark 7. Roll the second rectangle of pastry to increase the size a little more – by another 5cm (2 inches). Brush some milk around the margin of pastry and place the second rectangle of pastry over the top of the layered filling and gently press in the pastry sides, enveloping the filling. Turn over the edges of the pastry and seal the two rectangles together, brush the top with a beaten egg and put in 3 small diagonal slits. Bake for 10 minutes then reduce the temperature to 190°C, 375°F, gas mark 5 and bake for another 30 minutes or until it is a deep brown colour.

Cut into 6 (or 8) equal portions and serve warm with soured cream and chives.

SMOKED SALMON AND CREAM CHEESE BAGEL

INGREDIENTS

For 2 sandwiches:

2 Bagels – I've used a multigrain Bagel – if you see bagels with poppy seeds on top, even better, (or white rolls or croissants)

Butter – unsalted preferably

A little Dijon mustard

100g (4oz) Smoked salmon cut into ribbons 3cm (1 inch) wide

60g (2½oz) Cream cheese. Low fat and/or with chives

Some fresh dill

Freshly ground pepper

A wedge of lemon

A very simple, well known American breakfast for office workers. In America, there is a rather unsophisticated smoked salmon called 'Lox' which is very popularly used in a breakfast sandwich, usually served in a small, close textured ring-shaped bun called a 'bagel'. Smoked salmon has a huge range of qualities – the best being oak smoked Scottish or Irish wild salmon to smoked salmon off-cuts – bits of smoked salmon that is bought in a bag very cheaply. I would recommend you buy the mid-range stuff that is ready sliced and sold in 225g (ish) packets. Smoked Salmon is quite good for those on diets and needing less cholesterol. This is a good breakfast for those 'on the go' or for a picnic or desk breakfast.

METHOD

Cut the bagels (or rolls) in half and toast under the grill, butter both sides. Start to build the sandwiches: spread the cream cheese evenly over the bottom halves, lay the smoked salmon over the top and allow the ribbons to make even folds for presentation, grind a little black pepper over the top, just allow the top half of the bagel to lean, gently, onto the salmon and serve with a wedge of lemon. I like to put a few fronds of fresh dill in the sandwich for a little difference. I have also enjoyed a light spread of Dijon mustard on the top side of the bagel – it gives a little 'bite' to an otherwise quite bland sandwich.

If you want to pack the bagel for later, put the top half of the bagel on top (unfortunately you will lose the folded ribbon affect), wrap in greaseproof paper and store in the fridge for later. Keep the lemon wedge separate from the sandwich.

EGGS ST PETER

INGREDIENTS

For two people:

Hollandaise sauce: you will need a sauce blender or hand electric whisk is vital for this sauce

100g (4oz) clarified butter – melt un-salted butter extremely gently until the milky solids form in the bottom of the pan and you can pour off clear melted butter

A sprig of tarragon left in the melting butter to infuse some tarragon flavour

1 tablespoon of water

1 tablespoon lemon juice

1 yolk of egg

Salt and pepper

2 to 4 slices of good smoked salmon

300g (10oz) Spinach – remove the stalks

1 English muffin

2 large eggs

A couple tablespoons snipped chives to decorate

This is a dish similar to Eggs Benedict but with smoked salmon. It makes a light, Easter to summer breakfast or brunch and was introduced to me by a guest who didn't want ham or bacon with his Eggs Benedict.

METHOD

First make the Hollandaise sauce: Put into a cold bowl; the water and lemon juice, the egg yolk, salt and pepper, put the bowl over simmering water (don't let the water touch the bowel), with a hand-whisk (electric hand-whisk would be better), whisk the egg mixture to a 'Ribbon' consistency – where you can see ribbons when you lift up the whisk from the mixture – this will take about 5 minute of continuous whisking! Now, whilst continuing whisking, gradually add the warm clarified butter – take out the sprig of tarragon. Make sure the water in the pan is at a slow simmer and whisk until the sauce is like very thick cream or a light mayonnaise. Keep warm in a bowl over some hot – not boiling, water in a saucepan.

In a hot wok or large frying pan, melt a knob of butter and a teaspoon water, toss in the spinach and wilt down – just going flobby. Remove from the wok draining as much liquid as possible. Keep warm.

Toast the muffins and place them onto the plate, one half on top of the other and then fold the smoked salmon onto each of the top muffin. Put the ensemble into a low (heat) oven to warm the salmon up a bit, for at least 10 minutes. Don't allow the salmon to turn opaque.

Boil some water with a teaspoon or two of vinegar, in a small, shallow, non-stick saucepan or frying pan with a lid or plate to cover, or use a deep saucepan with lots of water. Crack the eggs into ramekins or teacups. Reduce the water to a slow simmer; pour in the eggs from the teacups gently into the water. Soft poach the eggs for 3 to 4 minutes.

Now build your Eggs St. Peter; you need to be swift to make sure it's hot. Take out of the oven; the muffins with the warm smoked salmon. Cover the salmon with the spinach. Take the poached eggs out of the water with a slotted spatula or spoon, one at a time, have a wad of kitchen paper ready on which you pat the slotted spoon and the egg to make sure all the water is off, (a 'Delia' trick!) lay the egg on top of the spinach. Spoon enough Hollandaise sauce over the eggs to cover - about a tablespoon or two; serve with a grilled tomato with chopped chives on top, or with a handful of dressed mixed-leaf salad for Sunday Brunch.

See recipe for Mock Hollandaise – a low cholesterol version – page 69.

BREAKFAST FISHCAKES

INGREDIENTS

For 8 fishcakes:

275g (10oz) Pollack, Gurnard, Cod or Haddock fillet – or any white round fish. The more types of fish, the more flavours you will get

225ml (8 fl oz) Full-fat milk

The rind (in one piece) and juice of about a ¼ lemon

A bay leaf and 20 turns pepper grinder

Handful of parsley chopped

A tablespoon butter

A little olive oil

1 Finely chopped white onion

350g (12oz) Mashed potato

Salt and pepper for seasoning

Flour

1 beaten egg

Half a loaf of white breadcrumbs or 100g (4oz) Japanese Panco

There is nothing better than a light fishcake to start the day. A 'breakfast' fishcake is simple and unfussy, with a light flavour and best served with a poached or scrambled egg:

METHOD

Put the milk, fish (that you have cut into smallish chunks), bay-leaf, lemon rind (that's in one piece), and the ground pepper, in a pan with a lid. Bring to a simmer for 2 minutes with the lid on. Pour in the lemon juice and remove from the heat. Remove the bay-leaf and lemon rind, and strain the whole lot into a mixing bowl and reserve the milk. Put the fish in another bowl. Remove any fish skin and bones you may find. Throw in the parsley and allow to cool a bit. Melt the butter in a saucepan with a little olive oil – to stop the butter burning and to add a little flavour. Fry the onions until they are translucent – do not allow the onions to colour. Stir in the mashed potato to warm up a little then the fish. Stir in the milk the fish was cooked in a bit at a time until the mixture is wet but firm. Season to taste and mix all the ingredients together with a wooden spoon off the heat. The fishcake mix should not be too dry, but, then again not too wet as to be difficult to form a fishcake. It is a fine balance to keep in mind when mixing in the milk. Whilst you allow the mixture to cool, season some plain flour with salt and pepper and sprinkle over the work surface. Beat an egg (with, perhaps a teaspoon of water) in a flat bottom bowl and breadcrumbs in a second bowl. Using slightly wet hands – to stop the mixture sticking to your fingers – form 8 small cakes or 4 big cakes in the seasoned flour, then egg-wash, then breadcrumb all 8/4 cakes. Leave on a tray for at least an hour (even better, overnight) in the fridge. Fry the cakes for about five minutes on each side very gently in a little butter and olive oil, or grill on a low heat for the same time.

Serve with a poached egg on top and Beurre Colbert (page 103) melted over the egg or with soured cream and chives on the side, as they do in Denmark.

SMOKED HADDOCK FISHCAKES

INGREDIENTS

For 6 people, 2 fishcakes each:

750g (1lb 11oz)Baking potatoes

500g (1lb 2oz) smoked haddock

500ml (17fl oz) full fat milk

A bay leaf

6 whole black peppercorns

2 heaped tablespoons of finely sliced spring onions

2 teaspoons of horseradish sauce

40g (1½oz) plain flour

1 large egg

Salt and freshly ground black pepper

Plain flour for dusting

Vegetable oil for frying. Vegetable oil makes the fishcakes crispier, however, if you want the cakes a little tastier, use ordinary olive oil

Smoked Haddock is fast becoming as popular for breakfast and Brunch as eggs and bacon. This is a relatively easy fishcake and can be made way in advance. Smoked haddock should be a plump fillet of fish, with the merest hint of a smoky yellow, running through the light greyish, nearly opaque flesh. Steer clear of the bright yellow stuff. Telly-chefs keep saying don't buy dyed smoked haddock and for some reason it is still sold in the supermarkets, so there must be demand for it! Has it not sunk in that there is little or no benefit to dyed haddock – unless you enjoy a slight metallic taste and, possibly disguised old fish!

METHOD

Bake the potatoes in a hot oven for about 45 minutes to an hour. When they are ready, scoop out all the flesh into a bowl and mash it up, you will need at least 500 to 600g of potato. Set aside and allow to cool.

Meanwhile; heat the milk in a wide, shallow saucepan or frying pan, with the bay leaf and peppercorns and then poach the fish when the milk comes to a simmer, for 4 to 5 minutes. Allow the fish to cool in the milk – until the fish is cool enough to handle. Remove the haddock from the milk and flake the fish in with the potato, taking care to remove the skin and any bones or peppercorns that might have escaped the milk. Add the spring onions, flour, horseradish sauce and a beaten egg, season well – quite a lot of pepper, not too much salt – and mix everything together well. Divide into 12 lumps and shape into fishcakes, helped with the dusting flour. It can be a little sticky so keep your hands dusted with flour. Refrigerate until you want to serve them.

Fry the cakes for 3 to 4 minutes on each side in a little oil until golden brown. Serve with some watercress, and a slice of Beurre Colbert (see page 103).

SMOKED HADDOCK BRANDADE AND CRISPY BACON

INGREDIENTS

For 4 people:

200g (7oz) mashed potato

200g (7oz) smoked haddock

1 bay leaf

2 cloves garlic, crushed with the flat of the knife

1 big slice zest of lemon; just peel off a couple of inches with a potato peeler

300ml (¾ pint) milk

Seasoning

1 tablespoon lemon juice

½ teaspoon Cayenne pepper

2 tablespoons fresh chopped chives

Salt and pepper

8 to 12 rashers streaky bacon

4 thick slices walnut bread

A kind of breakfast pâté. Smoked fish is not only very popular Brunch fare, but also it goes extremely well with bacon. The Brandades are served as 'quenelles' – this is a three-sided, lozenge shape and is very 'cheffy'! You achieve it by moulding a lump of pâté (or ice cream or mashed potato – anything like that) into a neat shape using a couple of tablespoons that have been dipped in hot water for lubrication. It takes a couple of attempts to get the hang of it. Send me an email (hugo@breakfastbook.co.uk) if you run into trouble and I will send you more explicit instructions. But persevere, its worth it for presentation.

METHOD

Pre-heat the oven 190°C, 375°F, gas mark 5.

Make the mashed potato if you haven't got any leftovers and keep it warm. Put the milk in a pan with the bay leaf, garlic cloves, piece of lemon zest and some salt and pepper. Bring gently to a simmer and just before it boils put in the fish. Push the fish into the hot milk to poach for about 4 to 5 minutes. Lift out the fish and remove the skin, don't discard the milk. Flake the flesh into a bowl with the mashed potatoes – keep an eye out for bones. Mix in three tablespoons of the poaching milk, lemon juice, chives and thoroughly mix the mixture into quite a fine pâté. Use the back of a fork. Add more milk if it is too dry. Cool in the fridge for at least an hour. To serve hot; shape the pâté into 8 'quenelles' – a three-sided lozenge shape – with two tablespoons. Place the 'quenelles' on a non-stick baking tray and place in a moderately hot oven to heat through whilst you cook the bacon or keep into the fridge to go cold. For health and safety reasons, if you are going to serve them warm, you must heat them up to quite hot after allowing them to cool. If you are serving them cold (in the summer for example) make sure you cool them for at least an hour in the fridge. They should not hang around warm for hours!

Put the streaky bacon on a roasting tray that has been brushed over with oil. Put into a very hot oven or under a grill for about 5 minutes. Turn the rashers over and grill or bake for another 5 minutes. Repeat this until the rashers are crispy. Put the crispy rashers onto kitchen paper and dab away any oil. They will keep crispy hot or cold.

Serve a couple of the quenelles to each person, with toasted walnut bread fingers, two or three rashers of crispy bacon and a chunk of lemon. After you spread the toast with the pâté, a little squeeze of lemon, take a bite and then a bite of bacon – fabulous.

PIPPAS KEDGEREE (GF)

INGREDIENTS

For 4 people:

450g (1lb) Smoked Haddock that has not been coloured yellow

Milk for cooking the Haddock

50g (2oz) Butter with a little oil for frying or Ghee - Indian clarified butter

2 Teaspoons medium curry powder

1 large Spanish onion, finely chopped

4 Hard boiled eggs – put the eggs into hot water, bring to the boil and boil for 6 minutes then immediately run cold water over them, this will enable the shells to come off easily. Allow to cool

225g (8oz) Basmati rice

More butter to serve

Freshly ground black pepper

Chopped coriander* or parsley

My wife Pippa is well known for her Kedgeree, we get requests for Kedgeree all the time from guests and it has been known for them to book only when Pippa has made this traditional breakfast dish. Originating in India during the time of the Raj, in the eighteenth century, it was called Khichri and was a particular favourite of the British.

METHOD

Place the haddock skin-side down in a roasting pan and cover with half milk, half boiling water. Put into a hot oven for 5 minutes until the haddock is cooked. Remove from the oven and allow to cool in the liquid. Meanwhile, melt the butter and the dash of oil (or use some Ghee), in a thick bottom saucepan over a medium heat. Stir in the curry powder and cook for 30 seconds to release the flavours. Now add the chopped onions and stir with the curry powder. Cook the mixture gently for 10 minutes then leave to one side to cool. Cook the rice to the instructions on the packet. After you have drained the water, and rinsed off any excess starch, spread the rice onto a baking tray a leave to dry in a slightly warm oven. Toss the rice every now and then.

In an oven-proof mixing bowl flake in the haddock, remove all the skin and as many bones as possible. Roughly chop the eggs into quite big chunks, the yolks will be still a little soft. Put in the dried rice and heat up the onion mixture a little and spoon it on top of the rice. Gently stir the Kedgeree together, cover with kitchen foil and put into a warm oven for 15 minutes to heat gradually through.

Serve with a knob of butter and chopped fresh coriander* or parsley and some Granary toast. *Fresh coriander is probably a little strong for breakfast so I would use parsley for your guests. People can be quite odd about fresh coriander!

SMOKED HADDOCK, BACON AND SWEETCORN CHOWDER (GF)

INGREDIENTS

For 4 bowls:

A knob of butter with a drop of oil

100g (4oz) Lardons or thick-cut smoked bacon chopped into small cubes/chunks

2 finely chopped Spanish onions.

675g (1½ lbs) main-crop potatoes peeled and chopped into little cubes

600ml (1 pint) milk

Salt and pepper

A bay leaf

500g (just over a pound) smoked haddock fillets – un-dyed

275g (10oz) sweetcorn (frozen is better than canned)

300ml (10fl oz) double cream

6 hard-boiled and shelled quails eggs

2 heaped tablespoons chopped chives and/or parsley

This is not a traditional Brunch or breakfast dish but I love it first thing on winters Sunday Morning after a long lie-in; when the weather is too awful to get up! Make the night before. It makes a very good supper, even a lunch – an 'All Day Breakfast'?!

METHOD

Pre-heat the oven 220°C, 425°F, gas mark 7.

In a large saucepan, melt the butter with a drop of oil and add the Lardons, fry until they start to brown then add the chopped onions and cook until soft. Now, stir in the potato cubes and 200ml (half a pint) of the milk and bring to a simmer and leave to simmer for 10 minutes, stirring every now and then.

Put the haddock into a flat oven-proof dish and pour in the rest of the milk and a couple of tablespoons of water, add the bay leaf and a little salt and some freshly ground black pepper. Place in the oven for 5 to 7 minutes or in a microwave – covered in cling-wrap with a couple of holes for vents – for 4 to 6 minutes. The fish should be just cooked and flaky. Take out the fish and remove the skin and flake the fish into the saucepan with the onions and potatoes etc, then pour the cooking liquid – the milk and seasoning – through a sieve in with the rest of the ingredients, adding the sweetcorn and cream bring to the boil and then reduce to simmer for another 5 minutes and then ready to serve. Lastly; gently stir in the quails eggs.

Correct for seasoning and then serve into bowls, sprinkle some chopped chives or chopped parsley over the top and serve with a large chunk of crusty, rustic bread. You can freeze this soup/stew but not with the quails eggs. If you make this the night before, make sure you cool it and refrigerate it overnight and very gently re-heat it in the morning. This means you can have another hour in bed.

COLD STREAM EGGS (GF)

INGREDIENTS

For 2 people:

A large kipper filleted weight about at least 225g (8oz)

4 Finely sliced spring onions

6 Tablespoons – about 150ml (¼ pint) double cream

4 Large eggs

Freshly ground pepper

An old favourite that needs to be revived for breakfast:

METHOD

Pre-heat oven at 180°C, 350°F, gas mark 4.

You need 2 large ramekins (225 ml – 8 fl oz) that have been thoroughly buttered on the inside. Place the kipper or kipper fillets in a roasting pan, cover with boiling water and put into the oven to cook for 2 to 3 minutes. Take the kippers out of the water but, don't throw the water away yet, and flake the meat into a bowl removing as many bones as possible and any skin. Mix in the sliced spring onions, two tablespoons of the kipper water and two tablespoons of the cream and mix gently with the meat. Fill the ramekins with the kipper mixture and make an indentation in the top of the mixture. Break an egg into the indentation and pour the rest of the cream over the top of each of the eggs. Season with just ground pepper and put the ramekins onto a baking sheet and place in the oven for 10 to 12 minutes. If the eggs have not set (if they are fresh eggs) place them in the oven for another 5 minutes, or until they have set to just runny.

Serve in the ramekins with buttered wholemeal toast.

Smoke me a kipper; I'll be back for breakfast!
Arnold Rimmer

HAM AND EGG BREAKFAST TART

INGREDIENTS

For 4 tarts:

You will need four 10 cm (4 inch) wide tartlet tins and quite deep – 2cm (¾ inch). I prefer the type that have removable bottoms

Pre heat oven 200°C, 400°F gas mark 6 and bottom left of an Aga

250g (8oz) Ready-made puff pastry

3 Cherry tomatoes cut into quarters

50g (2oz) Smoked, good ham (must not be watery, cheap ham)

2 Free-range eggs

1 Level teaspoon mustard powder

4 Tablespoons double cream

4 Fresh sage leaves or a teaspoon of dried sage

Salt and freshly ground black pepper

Pippa – my wife – says it is a Ham and Egg Quiche, I disagreed as I am not sure a Quiche is very breakfasty – also; 'men don't eat Quiche!' This is a portable breakfast – or a picnic breakfast, if you must eat breakfast on the move, this is just the thing. You can set it up the night before, make the pastry and roll it out and place into the tart cases, chop the ham etc. It is best to eat as soon as they come out of the oven or within a couple of hours.

METHOD

Butter the tartlet tins, roll out the pastry to about half a centimetre thick, using a 11½ cm (4½ inch) pastry cutter, cut out the pastry discs and line the tins, and cut little slits in the base of each tart-case. Set the cases onto a baking tray and leave them in a cool place or the fridge for at least an hour (this is why it would be good to do it the night before). Chop up the ham into little cubes and mix with the quartered tomatoes, equally distribute the ham and tomatoes between the tartlet cases. Beat together the eggs, cream, mustard powder and seasoning. Pour the mixture into the cases – don't over-fill – shred the sage leaves and push a few into the mixture of each tart. Place into the oven on the baking sheet for 15 to 20 minutes until golden brown. When you take them out of the oven, allow them to rest for a couple of minutes, remove from the tins. Serve hot or warm. If you cool the tarts down and refrigerate, you can serve them for the next couple of mornings by putting the tart (without the tartlet tin) onto a flat baking tray and putting into an oven at about 180°C, 350°F, gas mark 4, and heat up for 5 to 7 minutes.

This is a perfect tart for breakfast, not too many overpowering flavours. Alternative fillings are; smoked salmon and dill with the cherry tomatoes or for that European touch; Parma ham and Oregano and Sun-blushed tomatoes if you want the tart for a supper dish.

SAUSAGE, BACON AND EGG TERRINE

INGREDIENTS

To serve 12:

400g (14oz) un-smoked streaky bacon – at least 18 long rashers

600g (1¼lbs) Sausage meat

1 teaspoon each: White pepper and salt

2 teaspoons each: Dried sage, dried thyme

1 heaped tablespoon chopped fresh parsley

50g (2oz) ready-to-eat dried apricots. Chopped into quarters

50g (2oz) ready-to-eat pitted prunes. Chopped into quarters

3 small eggs – put into cold water, brought to the boil, boiled for 6 minutes, then plunged into running cold water. The yolks will be a little soft. If you prefer them harder, boil for 8 minutes. Any more and a grey layer will form in-between the yolk and the white. If you have your own hens with very fresh eggs, add 2 minutes

For a summer picnic Brunch. Served with home-made tomato chutney. I am hopeless at pickles as the process of cooking gets right up my nose – literally! I find Farmers Markets and Women's Institute sell the best delicious chutneys and piccalilli (also good with this Terrine). Or serve with fairy toast (see page 77) or a chunk of rustic wholemeal.

METHOD

Preheat oven 190°C, 375°F, gas mark 5.

Take a 2lb loaf tin and line the tin with the streaky bacon: First cover the bottom and the two sides with the bacon, then the ends, leaving a lot of the bacon spilling over the edge, so that you can fold it over the filling at the end. Overlap the rashers along the base of the tin a little.

In a mixing bowl; mix together the sausage meat, pepper and salt, the herbs, and the dried fruit. The best way to mix up the meat is to squidge it through your (clean) fingers until all the ingredients are thoroughly mixed.

Place a third of the mixture in the bottom of the lined loaf tin, be careful not to shift your beautiful streaky bacon arrangement. Describe a dent down the middle of the sausage meat mixture. Peel the boiled eggs, be careful not to split them, the yolks are still a little soft. Lay then lengthways along the dent in the meat. Pack more mixture along the sides and in any gaps and then over the top of the eggs and pat down the mixture so that it will fill all the gaps. Fold any ends of the streaky bacon down the side over the sausage meat and then flap the longer end pieces of bacon over to cover the bottom of the terrine. Cover with oiled tin foil and place into a roasting pan. Put the terrine and roasting pan into the pre-heated oven, fill the roasting pan with hot water to half way up the terrine. Bake for an hour. Remove the loaf tin from the roasting tin of water and leave to cool. When it is cool enough, place in the fridge. To serve, turn out the terrine out of the tin (put it into hot water for 30 seconds to release it from the tin). Turn it onto a plate and slice it into 2cm (½ inch) slices and serve cold, with some whole-grain mustard and a tomato, or what ever you choose.

SWEDISH BEEF AND FIG OPEN SANDWICH

INGREDIENTS

For each person:

A Slice of Pumpernickel bread

Unsalted butter to spread

A heaped teaspoon wholegrain mustard mixed with

A teaspoon runny honey

Seasoning

A handful of watercress leaves or rocket (no stalks)

Three or four, very thin slices of roast beef or air-dried ham

A ripe, fresh fig sliced thinly from pointed end to base

Not what us Brits think of as a breakfast or brunch, but something that is seen a lot in the Scandinavian and the Low Countries. Easily prepared and quite good for you. We enjoy this breakfast on a Spring Monday morning, it's quite useful if you had roast beef for Sunday lunch.

METHOD

Butter the slice of black bread – this is a heavy bread that is relatively easy to get hold of. Rye bread will do but should be toasted. Put on the watercress leaves. Fold the slices of beef in little folds, neatly on the watercress and spread over the mustard mixture and season with a little salt and pepper. Then arrange the sliced fig over the top.

Serve with grapefruit juice – the sourness of the grapefruit juice goes well with this breakfast dish.

I like children – fried for breakfast.

WC Fields

HAM AND ONIONS (GF)

INGREDIENTS

For 2 people:

2 tablespoons extra virgin olive oil

375g to 400g (14oz) small peeled shallots or onions (shallots are sweeter). Don't top-and-tail too much when peeling; keep as much of the stalk-end intact to hold the onions together

1 tablespoon Demerara sugar

Seasoning

4 tablespoons balsamic vinegar

A heaped tablespoon each: chopped fresh thyme or oregano and parsley

175g (6oz) air-dried, dry-cured ham like Denhay West Country Ham or Prosciutto Parma Ham

This is a lovely cold Summer Brunch and also a very old breakfast dish. I first had this Brunch dish when I was invited to Brunch organised by a group called 'Slow Food of Cornwall' – they are dedicated to everything that is not 'fast food' and have wonderful Brunches at lovely stately homes in Cornwall. You can see details about 'Slow Food' at the end of this book.

METHOD

Heat the oil in a saucepan (with a lid) and stir in the whole peeled onions (if they are quite big, cut them in half). Put on the lid and 'sweat' the onions over a gentle heat for 10 minutes. Add the sugar and season, cook very gently for 30 minutes. Add the Balsamic vinegar and the chopped herbs, bring to the boil and cook for a minute, stirring gently a couple of times. Turn the onions and the sauce into a bowl and allow to cool.

To serve: Spoon out the cooled onions and its sauce onto a plate, lay the ham in folds to one side of the baked onions. I enjoy this with a fried duck egg; the richness of the duck egg is cut through with the sharpness of the onion (very cheffy talk!).

THE GRADUATE'S BREAKFAST: FRIED BANANAS AND PEANUT BUTTER SANDWICH (V)

INGREDIENTS

For 2 sandwiches – I will leave it to you as to how many it will feed!:

2 Peeled large and ripe bananas mashed with a fork

2 Heaped tablespoons peanut butter - crunchy or smooth to your taste

4 Thin slices white bread – has to be white

100g (4oz)! Unsalted butter, or a low fat spread - but it never has the best effect

2 Tablespoons of jam or lemon curd or even runny honey - your choice - this is optional but is vital if you need the sandwich to ease a hang-over!

One of the great sandwiches, mostly for the young. Teenagers are addicted to this and it is so easy to make in a university campus kitchen. It is also a great way to use up over-ripe bananas. It is the kind of breakfast sandwich that will see you through the day.

METHOD

Spread peanut butter and the banana on two slices of bread. If the peanut butter is too hard warm it up a bit in a container of hot water or in a microwave for 30 seconds. On the other two slices spread the jam and sandwich onto the banana and peanut butter. Spread half the butter onto the outside of the two top slices. Melt a quarter of the remaining butter in a flat, heavy base frying pan over a low to medium heat – don't let the butter go black. Fry one sandwich on one side until golden – about 2 minutes, gently turn over the sandwich onto the side with the butter spread on and fry for another two minutes, or until brown. Add the last quarter of butter if needed. Repeat with the second sandwich. Serve hot with some Greek yoghurt and honey – don't eat anything else with calories that day!

He smiled rather too much. He smiled at breakfast, you know!

Charles Wheeler on the spy George Blake

VEGETARIAN SAUSAGES (V)

INGREDIENTS

For about 12 sausage-size
vegetarian sausages:

350g (12oz) Carrots –
peeled and sliced

1 Onion, small and finely sliced

Oil for frying

175g (6oz) Cheddar Cheese
(make sure it is vegetarian) grated

220g (8oz) White bread crumbs

Egg 1 large

Flat-leaf parsley 2 tablespoons
finely chopped

Fresh sage 2 tablespoons
finely chopped

Pepper

Flour for dusting

I do not approve of making carnivorous things, vegetarian; like vegetarian mince or burger etc. If you are a vegetarian, what is the point of having fake meat – why not just eat meat? I know there are a few people, like my daughter, who just hates 'red' meat. I make Vegetarian Sausages for my wife's vegetarian B&B guests. Many of them want the recipe, so, here it is:

METHOD

Boil the carrots in salted water for 10 minutes. Drain the carrots and allow to cool. Fry the onions gently for 2 or 3 minutes in the oil, don't allow the onions to colour, allow them to cool and put into a food processor with chopping blades along with the carrots and the rest of the ingredients (not the flour for dusting). Don't put in any salt as the cheese will be quite salty. Blitz the lot together to form a kind of dough. Turn out onto a work surface and divide into 12 lumps. Form each lump into a sausage and dust in flour, lay each sausage onto a tray and put them in the fridge for at least 30 minutes. You can freeze them at this point, individually wrapped in cling-film. Fry the sausages in a little olive oil and serve with Corncake (page 101) baked beans, baked mushroom and an egg of your choice.

IRISH SODA FARL (SODA BREAD) (V)

INGREDIENTS

For a loaf:

500g (just over a pound) plain flour

1 teaspoon granulated sugar

1 teaspoon salt

1 teaspoon Bicarbonate of Soda

225 to 300ml (over ½ pint) Buttermilk

25g (1oz) Melted butter mixed with 3 tablespoons buttermilk

This is not only an integral part of the 'Ulster Fry' (page 94) – a Brunch which is a heart murmur on a plate – but also a very good bread for serving on the side with jams and marmalade; a delicious morning bread and quite simple to make – no proving or 'knocking back'. One of the important ingredients is Buttermilk; this can be difficult to get hold of and there isn't an alternative, unfortunately.

METHOD

Pre-heat oven 190°C, 375°F, gas mark 5.

Sift all the dry ingredients into a large mixing bowl. To ensure you have mixed the bicarbonate of soda all the way through; sift it twice. Make a well in the centre of the flour and pour in three quarters of the buttermilk and gradually stir in the flour. Stir the mixture in the middle of the well with your fingers or a spoon and gradually draw in the flour until a dough forms. If the dough is too dry, add more buttermilk until the dough is soft and just a little tacky. Turn out onto a floured surface and knead for about 30 seconds, no longer. The Buttermilk will react with the Bicarbonate of Soda to make the bread rise.

Form the dough into a round loaf (about 20cm – 8 inches in diameter) onto a non-stick baking tray and cut into four quarters with a sharp knife – not quite all the way through or you will harm the tray. Brush with the melted butter mixed with butter milk and place into the oven and bake for 30 minutes. Brush some more butter and buttermilk after 15 minutes baking.

Check that the bread is baked by putting in a wooden cocktail stick and checking it is clean when you take it out. If it needs further baking, put back in the oven for a further ten minutes. If the top is brown, cover the loaf with foil.

To serve; tear the bread apart at the seam. Slice, toast or fry – pop an egg on top.

ULSTER FRY

INGREDIENTS

2 Eggs

4 Rashers dry cured bacon

2 Cookstown pork sausages (or ordinary, meaty pork breakfast sausages)

2 Slices Potato Bread (from the Ormo Bakery on the Ormeau Road) (I have used an Irish 'BOXDY' potato griddle cake – see page 96 I have no idea what Potato Bread is!)

1 Soda Farl (Ditto) [Soda Bread - Page 93]

3 Slices black or white pudding

1 Large frying pan

Beef dripping

1 Defibrillator

This is a contribution from John Smart; an Ulsterman who shares with me a love of Brunch, and an expansive waistline! These are his words, unedited:

[The bits in Italics and brackets are my thoughts on ingredients and cooking – if any. John is not known for classic cookery, and measurements. So please use this only as a guide] He says:

"There have been many great contributions to civilisation from the people of 'Nord Iron' but unique on the culinary vista is the "Ulster Fry" of which the "Full English" is but a pale imitation. Food has never been high on the list of priorities for the urban Province dweller – these are people, after all, who grew up with only 2 types of fish, white or brown.

"Irish minds are on more obvious forms of beauty, for example, no matter where you are in Belfast City you can see mountains, all you can see in England are buildings or flat fields you are not allowed to walk over, depressing even for a city boy like me [John Smart]. Belfast has the Black Mountains and the Antrim Plateau to the North and the Mournes to the South and they are truly dramatic; if it wasn't for the drink you would wonder how this location could spawn the fools it did. And then there are the Irish colleens – the nation is preoccupied with loyalty, treason, Guinness and the more mobile arts of drama and literature, food is truly only fuel.

"To prepare an Ulster Fry you require: [this should be for 2 people, however, I suspect John has designed this for only one substantial Ulsterman!]

METHOD

Fry the lot (in the dripping), you can butter the Soda Farl rather than fry, but only if Golden Cow butter is available. [I think you fry the bacon, sausage and slices of black pudding. I would fry the bread and potato Boxdy separately and place the fried eggs on top – well; that would be the English thing to do!].

"Serve with wheaten farl, [ordinary white bread 'doorstep-slice'] brown sauce, salt and gusto - Large pot of tea... must be Nambarrie, re-boiled on the stove. [Undrinkable thick builders-type tea].

"Alternative – for the gourmet/ health freak... no alternative"

[I was obliged, for reasons of research, to eat an Ulster Fry and found I did not need to eat again for at least two days!]

POTATO SCONES (V)

INGREDIENTS

Makes 12 scones;

500g (20oz) floury potatoes

50g (2oz) butter

100g (4oz) plain flour

Season as required

METHOD

This is a recipe from one of my readers of my Bed & Breakfast News magazine column. Carol and Gordon Bulloch have a lovely B&B call The Dulaig B&B, Grantown-on-Spey, in the middle of the prettiest bit of Mid-Scotland. I had a terrible time trying to design a Potato Scone; they were either rubbery and tasted like glue, or they came out hard and hollow and tasted like crispy glue; but Carol came to the rescue. It is easy; my recipes were too over complicated and silly! I should have listened to my own advice KISS - "Keep It Simply Simple". This is Carol's recipe – with a few suggestions from me in italics:

This will produce 12 smallish scones:

"Use 500g floury potatoes, mashed with a pinch of salt and 50g butter" *I put in a little ground pepper as well.* "Mix in about 100g plain flour – kneading a little with your hands if necessary, to form a dough – then roll out thinly on a floured surface and cut into triangles. Brown both sides on a hot griddle (or a thick-bottom frying pan). It is traditional in Scotland to fry the scones in butter or oil as part of a cooked breakfast: as I do not like greasy foods I prefer to eat mine [Carol] "dry" e.g. straight from the griddle or warmed in the oven, but for guests (and my husband [Gordon]!) I fry them lightly for about a minute on each side so they don't absorb much fat at all. I keep mine [Carol again] fairly small as our full breakfast [at The Dulaig B&B] is fairly substantial but give guests two if they say they have larger appetites.

Marriages are all happy it's having breakfast together that causes all the trouble.

Irish Proverb

BOXDY (IRISH GRIDDLE CAKE) (V)

INGREDIENTS

12 cakes:

225g (8oz) Grated raw potato

225g (8oz) Mashed potato

1 finely chopped fried onion (not traditional but needed, I feel)

225g (8oz) Plain flour

1 Egg

Plenty of salt and pepper

Milk about 100ml (4fl oz)

Oil and butter for frying

Perfect with an Ulster Fry (page 94). It is said:

"Boxdy on the griddle, Boxdy in the pan, If you can't make a Boxdy, You'll never get a man."

May not apply to some of us!

METHOD

Mix all the ingredients together with enough milk to make a stiff batter, thick enough to be reluctant to drop from a spoon. Heat a little oil and a knob of butter on a griddle or a frying pan. Drop a tablespoon of the mixture into the hot fat and fry on each side for 3 to 4 minutes. Serve 2 to each 'Ulster Fry'. I have added fried onions in the mix as I feel it needed a bit of a lift for our English pallets. I know an Irish cook will be shaking his/her head for this heathen addition, I sympathise; it's a bit like adding peas to a Cornish pasty, but not as bad!!

Only dull people are brilliant at breakfast.

Oscar Wilde

POTATO CAKES (V)

INGREDIENTS

For about 12 cakes:

300g small, roughly chopped boiled potato (for 10 minutes) or mashed potato. Make sure they are good, tasty, locally grown potatoes, English Whites, King Edwards or Marris Page

100g self-raising flour

1 teaspoon baking powder

50g melted butter

2 large eggs

Salt and pepper

A heaped tablespoon of chopped parsley and one of chives chopped

Vegetable oil for frying – could be olive oil but not extra virgin

These are the every-day, winter potato cakes, quick to make and very good with a full fry-up.

METHOD

Put all the ingredients in a food processor and blitz for about 30 seconds, or until everything is mixed together but not too fine. Heat a little oil in a frying pan to a hot heat and take a dessertspoon of the mixture and drop it into the pan. Leave to fry for a minute – or until little bubbles start to form on the top edge of the pancake and the turn the cakes over with a spatula and cook for another minute or two, until light brown in colour. Fry them four at a time. Serve almost immediately.

HASH BROWNS (V)

INGREDIENTS

To achieve crispy, flat, tasty Hash Browns for 2 people you need:

150g peeled and grated potato. Or, for extra fibre, scrub the potatoes and grate unpeeled

½ teaspoon salt

A couple of grinds of the pepper mill

A tablespoon beef dripping or goose fat or vegetable oil. Beef dripping offers a lot of flavour, goose fat will make a very crispy Hash Brown and vegetable oil is for those who are vegetarian. Olive oil will not get hot enough to produce crispy Hash Browns

Forget everything you might imagine a Hash Brown should look or taste. What you buy, frozen in the supermarket or (God help you) get in a certain Scottish hamburger 'joint' – bears no resemblance to a proper Hash Brown. It is so simple to make.

METHOD

Grate the potato onto a clean tea towel and sprinkle with the salt and mix the salt in with the potato and leave for it to think about life for a couple of minutes. The salt will draw out the moisture. Put the beef dripping into a small frying pan over a medium heat.

Whilst the pan is heating up, fold the edges of the tea towel over the potato; twist the ends of the tea towel clockwise one end, anticlockwise the other end to form a towel-cracker. Keep twisting until all the potato juice is squeezed out of the grated potato. Squish it with yours hands if you are strong enough. If you have squashed as much of the juices from the potato, turn the potato out into a dry bowl, add some pepper, increase the heat under the frying pan and put the potato into the frying pan. Spread out the potato so that it is flat like a pancake and fry for about 2 to 3 minutes or until the potato is turned a golden brown – lift the edge to check. Flip the Hash Brown over – either cut in half and use a spatula or toss it like a pancake and fry for another 3 or so minutes.

Serve with your favourite Brunch immediately or with a poach egg or anything that has lots of juices to mop up.

AMERICAN HOME FRIES (V, GF)

INGREDIENTS

This will be enough for four:

If you do not have any leftovers: cut up three or four medium peeled main-crop potatoes – about 450g (1lb) into 2cm (½ inch) cubes

Cut up a peeled, large Bermuda onion (red onion) into similar size cubes and fry with some oil and butter in a large frying pan, until soft and not quite brown. Meanwhile, boil the potato cubes for 4 minutes in 500ml (1 pint) beef stock (veg stock if vegetarian or plain, salted water). Drain the cubes

Everywhere in California (and probably, the rest of America) you can order 'Home Fries' to go with your (usually) vast breakfast. This is basically fried-up left-over potato with onions.

METHOD

Take the onions out of the frying pan and keep warm to one side. Season the potato cubes with salt and pepper and then fry in the same frying pan a few cubes at a time in more butter and vegetable oil (if needed) until brown.

If you do too many cubes at the same time they all turn into 'mush'.

Add them to the onions keeping warm until all is done. Put the whole lot back into the pan – now on a hotter setting – just before serving, to heat and to crisp up a little more. I must say – they don't ever get very crispy, if you want them crispier, put them in a hot oven on a baking tray for a few minutes with a sprinkle of vegetable oil.

BACON BUBBLE AND SQUEAK

INGREDIENTS

350g (12oz) King Edward potatoes (peeled weight) peeled and cut small

25g (1oz) Butter

Seasoning

25g (1oz) Butter and a little oil for frying

1 large Spanish onion peeled and fine diced

1 leek, cut in half, cleaned and finely sliced

1 teaspoon dried thyme

180g (6oz) finely chopped air-dried ham– like Parma ham or pancetta or cooked bacon

2 X 85g bags washed watercress – remove the thicker stalks

Salt and black pepper

I am sure you all know that Bubble and Squeak came from the noise that was made whilst frying this traditional English breakfast in the frying pan. This was created to use up the Sunday Roast leftovers – personally I prefer not to use leftovers but to make with fresh ingredients. I have also changed the traditional cabbage for leeks and watercress. If you just want a lovely Bubble and Squeak (as opposed to the 'Hash') just leave out the bacon and add corn beef. If you want an utterly traditional Bubble and Squeak, I am sure La Delia has a good recipe!

METHOD

Boil the peeled potatoes for about 20 minutes, drain them and return to the heat to get rid of any extra water. Add the butter and mash the potato, put the mash into a large mixing bowl with a little salt and pepper. Heat up the butter and oil in a non-stick frying pan – the bigger the better. Throw in the onions and fry for a minute; then the sliced leek and the thyme and cook for another 3 or 4 minutes or until they are about to turn brown, then add the chopped up watercress and cook enough to wilt the leaves a little. When they are done remove everything from the pan with a slotted spoon and put into the mixing bowl with the potato – allow to cool. Add the rest of the ingredients to the potato; ham, leeks and onions etc and mix together; put in the egg last – if the mixture is too sloppy don't put in the egg. You can either make about eight individual bubble and squeaks by putting the mixture into moulds, or chef's rings, in the hot frying pan three or four at a time. Or put the mixture into a frying pan and cook for about 20 minutes. Release the edge of the bubble and squeak with a spatula, place a plate on the bubble and squeak, with a well folded oven cloth over the top of the plate; flip the frying pan and the plate over so that the bubble and squeak ends up on the plate (hopefully it hasn't stuck to the pan). Slide the bubble and squeak back into the pan – uncooked side down for 5 to 10 more minutes.

Serve with a poached egg, brown sauce or piccalilli. It is just as enjoyable cold as it is hot – I love it with cold baked beans but I seem to be the only person in the world who does. Another thing I enjoy is to use cooked Brussels-sprouts and corned beef instead of ham with a couple of teaspoons of grain mustard.

CORN CAKES (FRITTERS) (V)

INGREDIENTS

For 12 Cakes:

110g (4oz) Self raising flour

1 Teaspoon baking powder

340g (285g net weight) Tin of sweetcorn nibblets

3 Eggs

Heaped tablespoon chopped parsley

Heaped tablespoon chopped chives

Salt and pepper

Vegetable oil for frying

A good summer 'extra' with your full English breakfast. The Americans call them Fritters.

METHOD

Put all the ingredients in a food processor and blitz for about 30 seconds, or until everything is mixed together but not too fine. It is nice to still have some whole corn kernels for texture. Heat the oil in a frying pan to a hot heat (not too hot) and take a level tablespoon of the mixture and drop it into the hot oil. Leave to fry for a minute and then turn the cakes over with a spatula and cook for another minute – or until light brown in colour. Fry them four at a time. Serve almost immediately with a full English or baked beans.

My wife and I tried two or three times in the last forty years to have breakfast together, but it was so disagreeable we had to stop!

Winston Churchill

KIPPER BUTTER (V)

INGREDIENTS

This recipe is for about 12 kippers, but it is kept in the freezer so that it can be produced to order:

Place into a glass mixing bowl:

250g (8oz) Soft butter

Tablespoon chopped parsley

The juice and zest of ½ a lemon

2 Teaspoons cracked red pepper-corns (or the mixed pepper-corns if the red are hard to find). Coarsely crack the corns in a mortis and pestle

2 Teaspoons horseradish sauce – the hot type, or 3 teaspoons of the cream of horseradish

Kippers are one of the breakfasts we, the Brits are most famous for, and, extraordinarily, virtually impossible to find anywhere else in the world. Try getting kippers in America – the country who have famously copied 'English' (as they like to call it) breakfasts and go to all sorts of lengths to serve English products – marmalade, English muffins, etc. This is a butter to serve with a kipper that brings out a lot of the flavours of the kipper.

METHOD

Mix the ingredients together with a fork until it is thoroughly mixed. This can be difficult as the butter will slip around the bowl with the lemon juice, but persevere and it will eventually mix into a creamy mixture. Spoon the mixture out onto a sheet of baking parchment paper (about 40cm – 16 inches). Spoon out in a row of lumps evenly across the paper and then smooth the lumps to form a long lump of about 5cm (2 inches) wide. Wrap the paper over the butter until it forms a kind of sausage-shape. Pinch the ends to stop the butter coming out. Put onto a flat surface in the freezer and leave for at least an hour.

To serve; put the kipper in a large jug of boiling water for no more than 2 minutes, or in a roasting tin of boiling water in a hot oven for a couple of minutes – no more. Slice a couple of half centimetre slices of the Kipper Butter on top. Slice a few slices straight from the frozen sausage and allow to defrost a little. Use a warm knife. It takes the butter quite a long time to melt over the kipper when it is frozen so it does not end up on the plate and hard to scoop up.

BEURRE COLBERT (V)

INGREDIENTS

250g (8oz) soft butter.

Tablespoon chopped fresh tarragon

Tablespoon of very finely chopped shallots – spring onions will do but only if you simply can't get shallots

The juice and zest of half a lemon

2 teaspoons cracked red pepper-corns (or the mixed pepper-corns if the red are hard to find). Crack the corns in a mortis and pestle, not too finely

METHOD

This is a traditional French butter served with fried fish, such as mackerel fillets, kippers or sardines.

Mix the ingredients together with a fork until it is thoroughly mixed. This can be difficult as the butter will slip around the bowl with the lemon juice, but persevere and it will eventually mix into a creamy mixture.

Spoon the mixture out onto a sheet of baking parchment paper. Spoon out in a row of lumps evenly across the paper and then smooth the lumps to form a long lump of about 5cm (2 inches) wide. Wrap the paper over the butter until it forms a kind of sausage-shape. Pinch the ends to stop the butter coming out the ends. Put onto a flat surface in the freezer and leave for at least an hour.

To serve; slice the butter into thick disks and place on the fish or fishcake to melt gently over.

GAVIN'S BLOODY MARY/ VIRGIN MARY

INGREDIENTS

For each glass:

Ice – fill the glass half full

Double shot -50cl Stolichnaya Vodka or a very good vodka. It has to be good to benefit from the strength

5 Good shakes of Worcestershire Sauce

A squeeze of lemon – about a ¼ of a lemons worth

Single shot - 25cl Chilli Sherry – this is a medium sherry with 'Birds Eye' chillis stuffed into the bottle and left to marinade for at least a week – or

Single shot - 25cl medium sherry and 3 to 6 drops of Tabasco

A good pinch Celery salt we think a ¼ teaspoon is a 'good pinch'

Tomato Juice to the top of the glass or, for something a little different, Gavin sometimes uses 'Clamato' Juice; tomato and clam juice with a few shakes of Thai Fish Sauce – it is just fabulous but not very helpful if you have a little too much the night before!

Stir the lot together. A stick of cucumber and/or celery for decoration

For Virgin Mary: leave out the alcohol, add 3 to 6 drops of Tabasco, squeeze in a little more lemon juice and add a heaped teaspoon of creamed horseradish

Gavin, who had a restaurant in Cornwall, developed his skill at the best Bloody Mary from nursing Fleet Street journalists for many years. It is, in my view, the best.

TOMARTINI

INGREDIENTS

For 2 Tomatinis:

6 cubes of ice

1 egg cup full of good vodka

3 egg cups of Tomato Water - Put 500ml (17fl oz) tomato juice through 3 thick, coffee filters. Leave to dribble through overnight. If you have room to do this in the fridge, all the better. It should yield about 250ml (9fl oz) of Tomato Water

2 teaspoons lemon juice

3 drops Tabasco

2 to 3 teaspoons egg white; (add a drop of water to the egg white, it makes it easier to handle)

I thank 'Captain' for coining the name of this Brunch drink. Tomartini is a sort of refined Bloody Mary that uses 'tomato water' as opposed to tomato juice. I got this idea from a 'Home Maker' program on American TV. I was trying to get up one morning after a long flight into Boston, USA for a holiday. I switched on morning TV, to the 'Food Channel' and there she was – Americas answer to Delia Smith; dressed in pink and peach, with a pink and peach work surface and bright green drapes (curtains) behind her, surrounding a fake Georgian sash window with plastic country views beyond. She was showing us how to make 'Tomato Water' "for a wonderful Brunch drink". This demonstration was constantly being interrupted by awful advertisements for cures for bodily inflictions such as 'Acid Reflux' (whatever that is), and Piles – on the food channel?!! Quite put me off my food – nearly.

METHOD

Place all the ingredients in a cocktail shaker. Put on the top of the shaker and shake vigorously for about a minute.

Pour through a cocktail strainer (keeping the ice out) into 2 chilled cocktail glasses with a stuffed olive to decorate. The egg white will produce a froth on top – if it does not get through the strainer, spoon some out onto the cocktail.

BULL SHOT

INGREDIENTS

In a blender per person:

Ice about 4 lumps

50ml (2fl oz) brandy

A tin of Consommé

One or two dollops tomato sauce/ketchup –
about two level tablespoons

6 Drops Tabasco

2 Teaspoons horseradish sauce (not cream of)

Juice ½ a lemon

Salt and pepper

Sometimes – for extra protein – an egg is
added

This is another 'cocktail' that is popular
with breakfasters or sufferers from
the night-before. I enjoy this as much
as Bloody Marys and, again, this was
revived for me by my friend Gavin, a
Fleet Street bar owner and master of the
Breakfast Cocktail.

METHOD

If the Consommé is good, it will be
slightly jelly-ish, you need to immerse
the tin in some hot water to loosen it up.

Blend the ingredient until the ice stops
rattling and serve in a tall glass with a
long spoon.

'BIN ON THE LASH'

INGREDIENTS

For a Smoothie for 2 people:

200ml (7fl oz) Orange juice

2 slices (about 200g – 7oz) fresh pineapple, remove the skin and the core, chop into chunks

A handful fresh basil leaves (about 10 large ones) - put a couple nice leaves aside for decoration. Home-grown basil will be stronger than the forced supermarket pots of basil. You will need half as much again of the shop-bought basil

The unlikely addition of Basil to sweet juices sounds incongruous, granted, but it is not dissimilar to the unlikely marriages of freshly ground black pepper with strawberries, chocolate with Chilli Con Carne or Nutmeg with a cup of cappuccino! All must be tried before condemned.

METHOD

Blitz the ingredient together with a handful of ice. Blend until you can't hear the rattle of ice. It will become a wonderful pea-green. Serve with a straw.

SAVOY HOTEL, BAR AMERICAN 'HEART STARTER' OR 'CORPSE REVIVER'

INGREDIENTS

In a shaker for each person:

35ml Brandy

35ml Ferniebranka

35ml Crème du Menthe!

Shake and strain into a cocktail glass, or drink it straight from the shaker – you are probably past caring

METHOD

I was told this recipe by the head barman of The Bar American in a smart West End Hotel. He has sadly gone to a better place and was one of the last of the 1920's type cocktail barmen. It is what was prescribed to party-people who needed something to start one up in the morning – if the thought of breakfast was too awful. I must say, the thought of drinking this would put me off getting plastered in the first place, but, I am told it is the best hangover cure - apart from a glass of Champagne! I can't say that I have ever had this 'cocktail' but, Gavin tells me it makes one 'very active!'

A 'SMOOTHIE'

INGREDIENTS

The basic ingredients: For 2 people - about half a litre:

A banana – an essential ingredient

A tablespoon porridge oats

150ml (¼ pint) Low fat yoghurt or full-fat

150ml (¼ pint) Skimmed milk or full-fat

A tablespoon of runny honey – you can change this depending what Smoothie you wish to create

2 or 3 Lumps of ice

A thick straw to serve

A Smoothie is a breakfast drink that will give you your morning wings; a meal in itself, it has wonderful 'good-for-you' properties and is very simple to create. You must start with the basic ingredients and then you can add all sorts of things to make a wonderful breakfast. It is very portable and can be drunk on your way to work.

METHOD

Put these ingredients into a blender and add anything that you would like to flavour the Smoothie:

A few (about 6) strawberries and (about 12) raspberries; mango (about half) and pineapple (about a quarter); 4 tablespoons of maple syrup and 12 pecan nuts, for example. A little apple juice will naturally sweeten the Smoothie. This is a great drink to experiment with and one to do with the children. It will encourage them to have breakfast if they are a bit anti-breakfast. As long as it is natural and fresh, you should not go wrong. A Smoothie helps digestion, a hangover and will give you a good boost in the morning, probably better than coffee!

SCARLET PASSION SMOOTHIE

INGREDIENTS

For a Smoothie for 2 people:

75ml Vegetable juice

4 Passion fruit – cut in half and the flesh and pips scraped out

125ml Cranberry juice

75ml Tomato juice

Juice of half a lemon

2 tablespoons chopped fresh tarragon

2 tablespoons honey (optional)

METHOD

Vegetable juice, Passion fruit, tarragon and tomato Smoothie. Now this is 'bonkers'!! But so good for you and a wonderfully unusual flavour. It has a rather passionate colour to it – don't get it down your 'Jammies'!

Blitz all the lot together with a handful of ice. Serve with a straw and slice of cucumber floating on the top and, perhaps, a lovely flower. A friend of mine suggested a cooked beetroot instead of vegetable juice would be different. I don't like beetroot but it sounds mad enough to be delicious. I shall however, leave it to you beetroot-lovers to try!

APRICOT AND STRAWBERRY CRUSH

INGREDIENTS

For 4 glasses (about a litre):

10 or 12 normal lumps if ice

6 or 7 Fresh apricots, stoned and simmered for 2 minutes in 150ml (¼ pint) water and a tablespoon of sugar

OR - pour in a small 400g can of apricots

250g hulled fresh strawberries

150ml (¼ pint) Fresh orange juice

1 Tablespoon honey if you need extra sweetness

A double measure (50ml) of Cassis or 50ml of Ribena for children

METHOD

A summer breakfast drink that the children will enjoy. Full of goodness, vits and fibre. This is not a very sweet concoction, but, with the addition of honey, makes it a little sweeter.

Blend until all the ice is crushed. Serve in a tall glass and a straw. With the addition of a couple of glasses of Italian sparkling wine, it is a summer drink the grown-ups will enjoy.

PEACH AND MINT FIZZ

INGREDIENTS

2 to 4 leaves of fresh mint

1 teaspoon caster sugar

1 large (50ml) Vodka

75ml (1½ measures - 3 fl oz) Peach Nectar

2 teaspoons lemon juice

Soda water

A refreshing morning cocktail. There is something about this drink that makes it taste quite innocent. The combination of innocence and alcohol makes it a very good morning-after–the-night-before drink, like a Bloody Mary. Perhaps I should have called it a 'Peach Mary'!

METHOD

Put in each tall glass:

2 to 4 leaves of fresh mint, rub them gently in your hand to bruise them, add a teaspoon of caster sugar, then a large measure or an eggcup of good vodka. Stir with a long spoon to infuse the vodka with the mint and sugar. Put in a straw or two and then fill the glass with ice. Add the Peach Nectar, the lemon juice, top up the glass with soda water (not sparkling spring water – it is not fizzy enough).

Garnish with mint tips (the only thing you should ever garnish with a Mint Tip, in my view!). If you want a non-alcoholic version, use half Cranberry juice, half Peach Nectar.

AROLO ITALIAN RED WINE

as told – by an Italian chef of note – the Italians enjoy a glass
this full, red wine with their breakfast.

ottle is opened on Monday morning and a glass drunk, then,
ving the cork off the bottle, a glass is taken each further
e mornings – six glasses altogether. By the time the bottle
inished on Saturday, the wine is wonderfully mellow and
icious. You don't, of course, drink Barolo on the Sabbath –
t Bucks Fizz!

he critical period in matrimony
breakfast time.

. Herbert

DEATH BY HOT CHOCOLATE!

INGREDIENTS

For two cups/mugs:

40g (1¾ oz) Milk chocolate

40g (1¾ oz) min. 70% Dark chocolate

300ml (½ pint) Full-fat milk – you could try semi-skimmed but, in my view, it is hardly going to affect the calories!

1 Egg yolk

2 Teaspoons Demerara sugar

Dark chocolate to grate over the top

The ultimate hot chocolate drink for the discerning chocoholic. It is rich and thick and velvety. Unfortunately, like most lovely chocolates, should be made only as a treat, in the morning or as a seduction tool!

METHOD

In a large metal (not non-stick) saucepan, melt the chocolate, broken into little lumps, in 2 tablespoons of water over a low heat. Pour in the milk when the chocolate is nearly melted (the dark chocolate will melt quicker than the milk chocolate, for some scientific reason). Using a sauce whisk (as opposed to a balloon whisk), whisk the milk and the chocolate together until all the chocolate has infused (if that is the word) with the milk. Keep whisking for a minute then leave to cook, very gently – not simmering or boiling – for 5 minutes before adding the sugar. Remove the pan from the heat and allow it to cool for a minute, then whisk in the egg yolk and return to the low heat and keep whisking for at least a minute more. Pour into the mugs and serve with some grated dark chocolate or ground cinnamon (I prefer the former).

For a little variety, put in half a teaspoon of vanilla flavouring (two drops of essence). Or for absolute decadence, whipped cream on top and a long spoon.

Serve with some Cinnamon Sticks (page 17).

DEATH BY CHILLED CHOCOLATE!

INGREDIENTS

For two people:

50g (2oz) Milk Chocolate

50g (2oz) min 70% dark chocolate

OR 100g (4oz) real drinking chocolate with at least 50% Coco solids

300ml (½ pint) warm full-fat milk – you could try semi-skimmed but, in my view, is hardly going to affect the calories!

2 teaspoons Demerara sugar

A teaspoon almond essence

25ml (1fl oz) orange liqueur (optional)

A large egg – as it is put in raw, not for 'preggers' ladies or vulnerable people (like sophisticated small children!) use a couple tablespoonspoons of double cream instead

This is NOT a milkshake and is not a drink for small children (unless they are very, very sophisticated small children – this is possibly a classic oxymoron!). This is similar to Death by Hot Chocolate but chilled and with the addition of an orange flavour. This drink is very fattening – there is no use trying to gloss over the fact. We slightly rotund people should only have it once a year, on one's birthday – or anniversary – or both.

METHOD

In a large metal (not non-stick) saucepan, heat the milk and put in the chocolate to melt, break it into little lumps, and do this over a low heat. Using a sauce whisk (as opposed to a balloon whisk), whisk the milk and the chocolate together until all the chocolate has infused (if that is the word) with the milk. Keep whisking for a minute then leave to cook, very gently – not simmering or boiling – for 5 minutes then add sugar stir it in until melted. Remove the pan from the heat and allow it to cool for a minute, then whisk in the Almond essence and orange liqueur.

To serve; put 6 to 8 ice cubes in a drinks blender, pour in the chocolate, doesn't matter if it is still a little warm, break in an egg and whiz up until the sound of the ice has stopped rattling. Serve with a straw and drink slowly – you are only allowed one!

INDEX

THANKS AND LINKS

My wife Pippa and all the staff at Woodlands Country House www.woodlands-padstow.co.uk for putting up with my mess, and Pippa's invaluable culinary assistance, doing most of the clearing up and giving me her honest (and invariably correct) opinion on each dish.

Rupert Wilson of Rick Stein's Seafood Restaurant (www.rickstein.com) for all his support for this book.

Head Chef Stephan of The Seafood Restaurant.

Stewart Paine – patisserie chef, extraordinaire!

David McWilliam of Bin Two (www.bintwo.com) in Padstow – for the back-drop for the drinks photos and his Smoothie contribution page 107.

John Smart for his Ulster Fry page 94.

Slow Food of Cornwall (www.slowfoodcornwall.com) for their inspirational, historic Brunch dishes.

Carol Bullock of The Dulaig B&B, Grantown-on-Spey for her help with Potato Scones (page 95). www.thedulaig.com

Ron Geach for his wonderful free-range eggs.

'Number One' in Padstow for all their help for the equipment for the photographs and:

Jane Watson Smyth for the use of her lovely Cornish farmhouse kitchen and huge selection of crockery for some of the shots.

Padstow Farm Shop for the ingredients for a great Brunch. www.padstowfarmfoods.biz

Johnny & Teri Walter for their support and the loan of their stylish crockery for photo shots.

Viki Carter (sister-in-law) from her B&B, Amerscot House Inn (www.amerscot.com) in Stow Massachusetts, USA – for some of the American contributions.

Adrian Oliver of Margot's Bistro www.margots.co.uk and Clair for their culinary contributions.

All my friends and family from here and abroad who have sent me ideas to be included in the book (some who made me include recipes in the book)!

Bob and Jo Hudson, and Sally Brown, et al at Hudson Armstrong for their design and artistry putting the book together (www.hudsonarmstrong.com).

Helen Minter for her efforts to ensure correct spelling and ingredients in this book.

Angela Rowe for her contribution to proof-reading this new book.

Mark Rushton & Helenka Bednar for their support and help from I Love My Grub (www.ilovemygrub.com).

Finally, to Rick Stein for his kind comments. Rick is a huge supporter of good food as you all know from his programmes. He has even included some of my recipes in his new book and magazine articles. He and Jill Stein are good friends and have always been very helpful with these books and even sell them in their wonderful delicatessen in Padstow. It is a huge advantage having the Seafood Restaurant 'machine' on your doorstep; when I get a problem with a recipe, I can get advice on dishes from some of the best chefs and cooks in the country (www.rickstein.com).

COOKING BREAKFAST

I know everybody who is capable of boiling water can cook breakfast – at least boiled eggs. Many budding cooks start their culinary experiments with breakfast – at the age of five, I tried frying Weetabix (a favourite cereal of mine) and serving it with scrambled egg (started off as fried but I broke the yolk and it ended up as a cross between an omelette and scrambled eggs with burnt Weetabix in it). It was delicious – I think, but I never cooked it again! With a little guidance from my mother (suggesting sliced bread being a better option to Weetabix) I never looked back.

Cooking a good breakfast is as vital as cooking a good supper, the quality level of a cooked breakfast and all the other elements of good breakfast, must be high. Breakfasts or Brunches covered in sugar, saturated in oil, too salty or, God forbid, tasteless, will put off people from indulging in the most important meal of the day!

The main thing to remember is to not go to excess – less is good, use the minimum of sugar and salt, you can always add more at the table. Fry in little, if any, oil. Bacon has its own fat and needs hardly if any fat to fry (if you have a good non-stick pan). Sausages need a little dob of oil and fried bread needs lots of oil, but if you get it hot enough, it will just fry the surface and not soak in to give you a heart murmur! And if you warm up some vegetable oil about half a bottle (about 350ml) in a saucepan to blood temperature, put in a good handful of fresh sage leaves and bunch of thyme leaves, into the oil and let it 'steep' in the oil for an hour. Pour the flavoured oil into a bottle (mark it 'Herb Oil') and fry your bread and potato cakes (page 97) in it for extra flavour.

Breakfast should be cooked with care. If you are too blurry-eyed in the morning, there is quite a lot you can do the night before and cook off the following morning. I told my son (when he turned a teenager) the facts of life and how to get along successfully in the world – not being wealthy (I am certainly not the person to advise on that!), but how to be popular and successful in life: (1) Play an instrument beautifully, (2) know how to be charming to people over 50 (especially to the mother of your girlfriend) and (3) to cook a wonderful breakfast or brunch! So, if, like my son, getting up before midday is a bit of a struggle, cooking the night before is useful. Like Grapefruit Granita (page 15) followed by Ham and Egg Strata (page 61) with Cinnamon Toast Sticks with the coffee (page 17) – the Strata and the Cinnamon sticks can just be popped in the oven whist you eat your Granita.

However, a freshly cooked breakfast is always well received, like freshly made coffee or just toasted crispy toast. I – and virtually everybody I know – hate flobby toast. At our B&B, guests are slightly surprised when they find they have to toast their own toast – but they appreciate it when they sit down to lovely crunchy toast. Why don't all hotels do that? Perhaps they do – some of them; none that I have been to.

Cook your breakfast as though you are cooking for a dinner party. No matter how small a breakfast you have – just toast and jam, for example – it should be homemade jam and bread fresh from the bread-maker. Nothing better than your own Granola (page 13) or for a smart Brunch; Eggs Sebastian (page 42) as stylish as you can get – and a Breakfast or a Brunch dish that you will never find even in the smartest Hotel in the world!

The equipment I have found most useful for Breakfast and Brunch cooking are: Apart from the obvious frying pans, spatulas, wooden spoons and non-stick saucepans etc; Chefs' Rings are – I feel – invaluable; they come in 2 sizes but I find the smaller, 2 ¾ inch wide by 1 ½ inch deep (7cm X 3.5cm) ring the most useful, for shaping Fishcakes or Bubble and Squeak etc. If you can't find Chef's Rings, a food tin-can, open at both ends would suffice. I like good tools like a pallet knife and metal spatulas with quite sharp ends so that it is easy to slip under the most delicate of eggs or Porridge Brûlées (page 20). A food processor is essential, as is an electric hand whisk; these help with bread kneading and sauce whisking, all the things that require a lot of elbow grease. I have a gammy right arm, so these are important pieces of equipment. Even if you don't have a gammy arm – these useful items will stop you getting one!